INDEX

ON CENSORSHIP

INDEX ON CENSORSHIP 6 1998

INDEX ON CENSORSHIP

Volume 27 No 6 November/December 1998 Issue 185

WEBSITE NEWS UPDATED EVERY TWO WEEKS
www.indexoncensorship.org
contact@indexoncensorship.org
tel: 0171-278 2313
fax: 0171-278 1878

Index on Censorship (ISSN 0306-4220) is published bi-monthly by a non-profit-making company: Writers & Scholars International Ltd, Lancaster House, 33 Islington High Street, London N1 9LH. *Index on Censorship* is associated with Writers & Scholars Educational Trust, registered charity number 325003 *Periodicals postage*: (US subscribers only) paid at Newark, New Jersey. Postmaster: send US address changes to *Index on Censorship* c/o Mercury Airfreight International Ltd Inc, 365 Blair Road, Avenel, NJ 07001, USA © This selection Writers & Scholars International Ltd, London 1998 © Contributors to this issue, except where otherwise indicated

Subscriptions (6 issues per annum)
Individuals: UK £39, US $52, rest of world £45
Institutions: UK £44, US $80, rest of world £50
Speak to Syra Morley on 0171 278 2313

This issue was proposed and co-edited by Ole Reitov from the Danish Broadcasting Corporation and Marie Korpe, project director of the first World Conference on Music and Censorship; Copenhagen 20-22 November 1998
Index has made every effort to arrange usage permissions for all copyright lyrics used within this issue – where we have been unable to arrange such permissions we believe we have made every possible effort to contact copyright holders. Our apologies to those we could not locate.

EDITORIAL

Censorship? What censorship?

Working on this issue of Index, one could be forgiven for thinking that suppression of music is one of the world's best kept secrets. Yet, as Index reveals, music censorship is alive and well, in many places and under many guises.

The subversive nature of music has long been recognised by rulers, religions and moralists. Plato condemned the use of specific intervals; William Byrd risked his life by composing music in secret for the Roman Catholic Church; Verdi had to tailor his libretti to avoid political censorship. What is the particular threat that music poses? Probably that its meaning is ambiguous and that its power gives dignity to people in awful predicaments. Whatever the cause, it is in our own 'beautiful, pitiful century', as Osip Mandelstam called it, that the censoring of music and musicians, from Shostakovich to Marilyn Manson, has particularly flourished.

Some parts of this story are familiar: the brutal racial and anti-modernist policies of the Nazis; Stalin's vicious campaigns against 'formalist' music. But how much is known of more recent stories – the silencing of the Mauritanian television star Malouma Mint Maideh, the killing of Lounès Matoub, the outspoken voice of Berber culture in Algeria, the multiple arrests of Fela Kuti for his oppositional songs in Nigeria, China's fear of 'spiritual pollution' by Western pop groups? Not to speak of events culturally closer to home – the criminalisation of dance culture in the UK through the Criminal Justice Act, the faith-propelled campaigns against rock music by the fundamentalists of America, the list of songs which were 'treated with caution' by the BBC during the Gulf War.

Meanwhile, the pop music industry's obsession with the bottom line (which, among other things, prevented Index from including some significant tracks on our CD) exerts its own pressures on musicians to adapt to cultural and political norms: no one knows better than musicians the particular pains of self-censorship.

Music is probably the most censored of all art forms. We report on how musicians are silenced, and the range of motives which silence them – power, piety, greed, fear and hatred – in fact, all the usual suspects. ❑
Ursula Owen, Marie Korpe, Ole Reitov

In conjunction with this issue, Index has produced a 55-minute CD of banned popular music; presented, together with Simon Rattle, a concert of banned classical music at the Union Chapel, Islington on 16 November; and is participating in the first world conference on music and censorship in Copenhagen on 20-22 November.

contents

Smashed Hits: the censors and the microphone

Tales of Terezìn: music the Nazis couldn't silence

Smashed Hits

Disc Notes

Index's first ever foray into the recording business could turn out to be its last. Creating this issue's cover-mounted CD, has been a learning experience in every way. First, discovering the sheer volume of music, and the multiplicity of styles and forms, that have been and are being banned.

Second, recognising in the protestations of chain stores, radio stations, consumer groups and governments the same old twisted logic of censorship: the all too familiar prejudice, the cultural blinkers, the violent intolerance we find in other, more closely observed spheres of censorship.

And third, discovering that for the majority of the world, the music censorship they experience now, unlike notorious occasions in the past, is not generated by intolerant governments, bigoted religions, over-zealous consumer watchdogs. The bodies that seek to exclude radical new music, political music that challenges convention and seeks to *change* things, base their decisions on greed. The biggest censor is the music industry itself, and its sole criteria is cash.
FF

1)The Tibetan Singing Nuns: The view from Drapchi prison
All the nuns singing on this track were jailed for taking part in pro-independence demonstrations in Chinese-occupied Tibet. The tracks used on this CD are taken from 'Seeing Nothing but the Sky', secretly recorded in prison. It is available from the Free Tibet Campaign, 9 Islington Green, London N1 2XH (44) 171 359 7573. Track licenced by kind permission of the Free Tibet Campaign

2)Crass: Bata Motel (Crass)
Boots and HMV in the UK refused to stock Crass's album. In 1984 a record shop in Cheadle was prosecuted under the Obscene Publications Act for stocking their records (among others). Crass helped to fund the subsequent appeal at which the only record against which the original verdict was upheld was the Bata Motel track from their Penis Envy album. Crass was an overtly anarchist band and it is very hard to avoid the conclusion that their constant harassment by the authorities was politically motivated. Track licenced by kind permission of Crass

3)Malouma: Maghrour (Malouma Mint Maideh)
Malouma Mint Maideh sings of love and sensuality in a country that spans the boundaries of the Arab and African worlds, worlds that frown on feminine empowerment. Maghrour's overt sensuality is a prime example of Malouma's erotic expression. Her songs are banned from national TV and radio. Track licensed by kind permission Shanachie Entertainment Corp.

4)Fela Kuti: Sorrow, tears and blood (Fela Kuti)
Fela Ransome (Anikulapo) Kuti was probably the most globally acclaimed African musician of the 20th Century. His music reflected his opposition to the brutality of Nigeria's many military regimes. Nowhere is this more visible than in the lyrics of Sorrow, Tears and Blood. Repeatedly jailed, Fela never stopped singing. Track licensed by kind permission M.W.F. Ltd.

5)Ian Dury: Spasticus Autisticus (Dury)
Nervous BBC bosses pulled the track for fear of causing offence - there are some subjects that aren't considered suitable for popular music, even a track written for the Year of the Disabled by a disabled musician. Dury sings right from the heart, a proud and savagely funny rebel song for all who don't fit. Track licenced by kind permission of Polydor

6)Eric Donaldson: Stand up (Donaldson)
Eric Donaldson, a Reggae star from Jamaica was responsible for writing Stand Up, a tune that became a clarion call in the black South African townships and was banned from airplay on mainstream South African radio. Track licenced by kind permission Serengeti Records.

7)Mzwakeh Mbuli - Freedom Puzzle (Mzwakeh Mbuli)
Mzwakeh Mbuli became known as the peoples' poet after reciting his poetry at high profile funerals during the Apartheid era. His stature was such that he was asked to recite at the investiture of President Mandela. His commitment to highlighting corruption in South African politics continued and he discovered a guns and drugs smuggling ring involving top South African officials. However, before he could make his discovery public he was arrested on charges of armed robbery, charges that many believe are fabricated. Mzwakeh is currently on remand and maintains his innocence from prison. Freedom Puzzle displays the consciousness of Mzwakeh's lyrics and his cynicism at the new South Africa. Track licenced by kind permission CCP Records. It is available on the album Kwazulu Natal from Sterns African Music Centre.

8)Flannel: Gravy Train (Flannel)
Flannel are Brighton 'agitpoppers' – musicians and political activists intent on blurring the line between performance and protest. In keeping with that, three of their gigs have been cancelled by the police, who view their music as incitement. Brighton police have also accused them of attracting 'drug users, anarchists and an undesirable element' to their gigs; local pub licencees have been threatened with the loss of their licences if they book the band. This track was distributed free at the industry's Brit Awards as a dig at the biz and Oasis. Track licenced in a drunken haze by Flannel/Dome Discs.

9)Exodus: Two thumbs (Exodus)
Exodus are a sound system collective who have, for the last decade, used music as a unifying force: squatting and restoring derelict buildings and providing training for the local community, as well as putting on blistering free parties. They're based in Luton, where town and county councils approve of their work. However, since day one, the local police have persecuted and harrased them, constantly raiding parties and Exodus buildings, bringing trumped up charges, including murder, against Exodus members. No serious charges have been proved in court. Luton council have called for a public inquiry into police behaviour and the Police Authority, who in law control the county police force, appealed to then Home Secretary Michael Howard to restrain the police. Track licenced 'for the struggle' by Exodus.

10)Hawkwind: Urban Guerilla (Dave Brock/Bob Calvert)
The follow-up single to their 1972 smash Silver Machine, this was to have been another heavily promoted single that should have clinched the band's international position. Good pre-release orders and airplay were turned upside-down when the IRA began a mainland bombing campaign. Within days the BBC pulled the track completely; deprived of airplay, Hawkwind management bowed to the inevitable and deleted the single.
Track licenced by kind permission EMI/Emergency Broadcast System

11)The Tibetan Singing Nuns: Rid the holy land of Tibet of the Chinese
Track licenced by kind permission of the Free Tibet Campaign

Index on Censorship owes a great debt of gratitude to the following people whose belief in the true accessibilty of music made this CD possible: Randall Grass at Shanachie, Irving Schlossberg at EMI(SA), Sean Watson at CCP(SA), Rikki Stein at MWF Ltd. Special thanks to Trevor Herman at Sterns/Earthworks, Martin Howell at Serengeti Records and Andrew King at Mute who all helped us to make the right connections. We are also grateful for the support of Doug Smith & Dave Brock, Nova, Ian Dury, Cosmo & all at Flannel, Glen Jenkins & all at Exodus. Index would also like to acknowledge the hard work put in by Tony Callaghan, and by Stig and Andy at Furry Dice.

Smashed Hits

Rhythm and Blues, Birmingham, 1998 – Credit: Nick Cobbing

JULIAN PETLEY

Though its trials are less monitored and recorded, music is no less subject to censorship than other forms of artistic expression, and the methods are much the same. These run the usual gamut from killing or imprisonment to banning the works themselves, and thence into that nebulous domain in which 'taste' and market forces are the engines of restriction.

One of the best-known musicians this century to have encountered the ultimate form of censorship – state-sanctioned murder – was the Chilean folksinger Victor Jara. Politically-infused popular song (*nueva canción*) emerged in Argentina in 1962 but soon became a potent force in the liberation movements then sweeping South America. It even found echoes in a Spain still labouring under the Franco dictatorship.

But it was in Chile, thanks to Jara and others such as Violeta

Parra, that it reached its peak; *nueva canción* played a key role in the campaign that led to the election of the Popular Unity government of Salvador Allende who, after the election, appeared surrounded by musicians with a banner proclaiming 'there can be no revolution without songs'. For Jara, 'the authentic revolutionary should be behind the guitar, so that the guitar becomes an instrument of struggle, so that it can also shoot like a gun'. His songs were in trouble before Allende was elected, and it is hardly surprising that when the democratic government was violently overthrown, Jara should have been one of the earliest victims of the brutal, US-backed dictatorship that succeeded it. Indeed, *nueva canción* was so identified with Popular Unity that General Augusto Pinochet's regime banned as subversive even the traditional instruments on which it was played as well as the works of all musicians associated with it. It was made an offence even to mention Jara's name.

Nor was the explicitly political persecution of musicians confined to Chile. Wherever the military was in power in the 1960s and 1970s, in Europe as in Latin America, popular resistance through music was stamped on. The Brazilian military coup of 1964 ushered in 20 years of military rule and, with it, strict censorship of broadcast music – and especially of *musica popular brasileira*. Numerous musicians during that period spent time in exile, including Chico Buarque, Gilberto Gil and Caetano Veloso. The 1967 military coup in Greece led to the imprisonment and torture of internationally known singer Mikis Theodorakis. Eventually he was released as a result of international pressure and went into exile; other, less well known musicians were not so fortunate. In Turkey, where the army still pulls the strings behind the civilian government, the Kurdish language is illegal, Kurdish music is banned from the airwaves and its singers, like Sivan Perwer and Temo, live in exile.

The most obvious example of musical censorship on the African continent, was for many years the apartheid regime in South Africa. But there are others. Fela Kuti encountered difficulties with almost every Nigerian government after independence; before it fell in 1991, the Mengistu regime in Ethiopia drove many musicians into exile with 'a censorship as pedantic as it was bureaucratic'; in Zaire, one of the greats of Congolese/Zairean music, Franco Luambo Makiadi, the leader of OK Jazz, was jailed on a number of occasions and had several records banned by the Mobutu regime, even though he was a crucial part of its *authenticité* programme.

In Islam too, despite the magnificent musical traditions of many Muslim countries, music and fundamentalism are all too often unhappy bedfellows. In Sudan under the National Islamic Front government, in Afghanistan of the Taliban, in Algeria where singers have been a target of Islamists and government alike, silence has fallen.

But there is little doubt that the most thorough-going and systematic attacks on music this century have been in the Soviet Union between 1932 and 1953, and in the Third Reich. Although these were by no means confined to classical music and composers, the latter bore the brunt of the attacks and it is for this reason, maybe, that they have received more substantial critical attention than popular music.

In Stalin's USSR, the chief enemy was modernism, or 'formalism' as it was usually known. From 1932, the doctrine of Socialist Realism, which had been developing for some time, became the Party line. In 1934 the newly formed Composers' Union stated that:

> 'The main attention of the Soviet composer must be directed towards the victorious progressive principles of reality, towards all that is heroic, bright, and beautiful. This distinguishes the spiritual world of Soviet man and must be embodied in musical images full of beauty and strength. Socialist Realism demands an implacable struggle against folk-negating modernistic directions that are typical of the decay of contemporary bourgeois art, against subservience and servility towards modern bourgeois culture.' (Quoted in Boris Schwarz, *Music and Musical Life in Soviet Russia 1917-1970*).

But it was not until 1936 and the premiere of Shostakovich's opera *Lady Macbeth of the Mtsensk District* that the storm broke in the form of an unsigned – though allegedly by Stalin himself – article in *Pravda* signalling a drastic intensification of the campaign against 'formalism' in *all* the arts. The opera was hastily withdrawn and, along with Shostakovich's recently completed but unperformed Fourth Symphony, silenced for a quarter of a century.

At the end of World War II, there was a further tightening of ideological and artistic control. Music's turn for the flame-thrower came in January 1948 when Andrei Zhdanov, chairing the First Congress of the Union of Soviet Composers in Moscow, identified 'formalism' with 'decadent western influences' and 'bourgeois cultural decay'. In a

resolution published the following month, the Party's Central
Committee attacked the leading composers of the day – Miaskovsky,
Prokofiev, Shostakovich, Shebalin, Popov and Khachaturian – and
defined 'formalism' as 'the cult of atonality, dissonance and disharmony'
and 'confused, neuro-pathological combinations that transform music
into cacophony, into a chaotic conglomeration of sounds'. It dismissed
everything by these composers as 'alien to the Soviet people' with
devastating consequences for them all. In some cases, it undoubtedly
contributed to their premature deaths. The contagion spread into other
countries under Soviet domination, restricting the careers of composers
such as Witold Lutoslawski in Poland and Gyorgy Ligeti in Hungary.

In the Third Reich, the enemy was again modernism, now coupled
with 'musical bolshevism' and Jewish influences, both real and imagined.
Thus Alfred Rosenberg, one of the Reich's chief ideologues, declared in
1935 that 'the atonal movement in music is against the blood and soul of
the German people', and the musicologist Herbert Gerigk in his *Lexicon
der Juden in der Musik* argued that: 'The twelve-tone system in music is
equivalent to Jewish levelling-down in all matters of life ... This
represents the complete destruction of the natural order of notes in the
tonal principle of our classical music.' The clearest example of this kind
of 'thinking' was provided by the *Entartete Musik* exhibition in
Düsseldorf in 1938; opening the event, its organiser, Hans Ziegler, stated
that it 'presents a picture of a veritable witches' sabbath portraying the
most frivolous intellectual and artistic aspects of Cultural Bolshevism ...
and the triumph of arrogant Jewish impudence'

However, anti-Semitic and reactionary musicology well pre-dated
1933. Wagner's essay *Das Judentum in der Musik*, which argued that Jews
are capable only of imitation rather than originality, had long ago helped
to make anti-Semitism respectable in the music field, and also helps to
explain why his music still cannot be publicly performed in Israel.

Specifically Jewish 'internationalism' was attacked in 1920 by the
composer Hans Pfitzner, who, ironically, also equated the 'atonal chaos'
of modern music with 'bolshevism'. In 1925, the renowned journal the
Zeitschrift für Musik was relaunched to campaign for the 'spiritual renewal
of German music' and became openly anti-Semitic. The *ZfM* was part
of the growing right-wing campaign against jazz and, like other
conservative musical forces, was particularly enraged by Ernst Krenek's
1927 opera *Jonny spielt auf!* Altogether unsurprisingly, Alfred Rosenberg

took up the same refrain in his paper the *Volkischer Beobachter* and in the *Kampfbund für deutsche Kultur* which he founded in 1929.

When the National Socialists won a majority in the local state elections in Thuringia in 1930; an 'Ordinance Against Negro Culture' was passed in order to rid the province of 'all immoral and foreign racial elements in the arts', all jazz was banned and works by Hindemith and Stravinsky were removed from the repertoires of state-subsidised orchestras. By now it was not uncommon for the Nazis to disrupt musical performances of which they disapproved; thus the Brecht/Weill *Mahagonny* encountered difficulties in Leipzig and Frankfurt in 1930.

In 1932 an SS *Untersturmfuhrer*, Richard Eichenauer, published *Musik und Rasse*, a work that was to be highly influential in the Third Reich, arguing that any racial mingling posed a threat to the supposed 'purity' of Nordic artistic achievements and needed to be stopped at all costs.

What those costs were became clear soon after the Nazi seizure of power. With the formation of the *Reichsmusikkammer* (RMK) as part of the *Reichskulturkammer* (RKK), whose president was Goebbels himself, it was relatively easy to purge the musical world. If composers and musicians wished to work they had to be members of the RMK, and membership was simply refused to 'undesirables', in particular to Jews, whose work was simply expunged from the broadcast and concert repertoire. Anti-Semitic measures were extended to cover Jewish music teachers and concert agents, and were greatly aided by the infamous civil service law of April 1933, which removed Jews from all areas of public administration, and the 1935 Nuremberg Laws which effectively banned mixed marriages. As part of the process critics, musicologists and radio personnel had also to join (if permitted, of course) the appropriate chambers of the RKK. The inevitable early exodus included the composers Kurt Weill, Hanns Eisler, Arnold Schoenberg and Hans Schreker, and the conductors Fritz Busch, Bruno Walter, Otto Klemperer and Hermann Scherchen.

It would be comforting to think that music censorship didn't take place in democratic societies. Comforting but, unfortunately, quite wrong. Musicians as well as the denizens of Hollywood felt the force of the McCarthyite witchhunts and the House Committee on Un-American Activities, no-one more so than Paul Robeson.

Robeson is undoubtedly the most censored of all American musicians. As Eric Bentley states in *Thirty Years of Treason*,

'[He] provided the American Establishment with the opportunity to see if it, like the Soviet authorities, could make an unperson of someone. In American history it would be hard to parallel the blackout of Robeson imposed by the Government and the press during the early and middle 1950s. It was as if the "famous actor and singer" had never existed.'

After years of harassment and vilification, the State Department revoked Robeson's passport in 1950, and US officials prevented him from singing in Canada in 1952. He was subpoenaed by HCUA in 1956 and put up one of the most spirited defences of any of those dragged through this charade. His passport was eventually returned, after strong international pressure, in 1958. There is no doubt, however, that like some of the Soviet composers, the experience of political persecution left him a broken man.

In the UK, meanwhile, it was US music that was causing problems and being rationed by the cultural authorities to the point of censorship. When rock'n'roll arrived in Britain it encountered a strictly controlled popular music regime: of the three BBC radio stations only one, the Light Programme, played pop, and the BBC restricted its 'needle time' (programming of records) to 22 hours a week across all three channels. Deeply uneasy about the growing teenage phenomenon and worried about the 'Americanisation' of British youth, the BBC consciously resisted rock'n'roll and deliberately favoured less-threatening British alternatives, such as skiffle and Cliff Richard. The attitude of the music press, which consisted of only the *New Musical Express* and *Melody Maker*, was equally censorious and was typified by a 1956 article in the latter by Steve Race in which he complained that 'viewed as a social phenomenon, the current craze for Rock-and-Roll material is one of the most terrifying things to have happened to popular music'.

The BBC may have given up patrolling the parameters of popular musical tastes, but the years since are nonetheless littered with examples of banned and marginalised records which suggest that, for the Corporation, music is still a potentially subversive force. At one time or another, worries about drug references and sexually explicit language have banished from the airwaves songs by some of the biggest groups, including the Beatles and the Rolling Stones. Various chapters of the Irish 'Troubles' have involved the temporary disappearance of a range of 'politically sensitive' material; 'unpatriotic' lyrics became casualties of the

Falklands/Malvinas and Gulf wars; songs on the Queen, Margaret Thatcher and Ronald Reagan have equally been victims of the desire not to offend.

This list of bans, however, is not only far from complete, it ignores a much more everyday, taken-for-granted form of control. As John Street puts it in *Rebel Rock*, 'what is of greater concern are the records that disappear before they even reach the public. It is radio's and TV's ability to act as a gate-keeper for public taste that identifies the real site of political control'. The key mechanism here, in the case of both the BBC and the commercial stations, is the playlist which, in selecting those records to be played, automatically excludes many others and thus plays a crucial role in setting the musical agenda.

Radio and television are not, however, the only censors. In 1977 the title of the album '*Never Mind the Bollocks Here's the Sex Pistols*' was the subject of an unsuccessful prosecution in Nottingham under the Indecent Advertising Act of 1899 and, in London, the Small Wonder record shop was raided for stocking it. In 1982, after pressure from Mary Whitehouse's National Viewers and Listeners Association, the Anti-Nowhere League's 'So What' became the first record to be successfully prosecuted under the Obscene Publications Act. Two years later this was joined by the 'Bata Motel' track from the album 'Penis Envy' by Crass.

By refusing to stock certain items, major record shops also act as censors, although doubtless they would argue that they were simply exercising 'normal commercial judgement' or something equally euphemistic. In 1987 the *New Musical Express* revealed that HMV had drawn up an extensive Obscene Product list of records that would not be stocked in their outlets.

Of course, HMV are not alone in acting thus. Indeed, when the major chain WH Smiths banned the Sex Pistols' 'God Save the Queen' some branches effectively made it a 'non-record' by leaving a blank in their singles' chart where it should have been. Records carrying stickers warning of 'explicit lyrics' put certain chain stores immediately on their guard and, according to Martin Cloonan in *Banned: Censorship of Popular Music in Britain: 1967-92,* the ubiquitous high street chain Boots refuse to stock such products altogether as 'we do not consider it ethical to stock merchandise which would offend the families that shop at Boots'. Presumably they don't consider it economic good sense either, and this is where market forces once again enter into the censorship process. The stickering of records, which originated in the States as a defensive response by record companies to campaigns by the Parents' Music Resource Centre, is not simply a matter of 'consumer protection' but actively contributes to the marginalisation, demonisation and, ultimately, censorship of certain kinds of records.

The suspicion that the treatment of such records is, in the broadest sense of the word, *ideologically* motivated is intensified if one examines it in conjunction with the sustained and, on occasion, brutal persecution of the New Age Travellers, in whose culture music plays a central, defining role, in the UK during the 1980s. While groups such as Liberty were demanding public inquiries into the abuse of power and illegal police behaviour, the government was busy urging local authorities to use all available existing legislation, however arcane, against the travellers, and enacting new measures such as the 1986 Public Order Act, the 1990 Entertainments (Increased Penalties) Act and, most important, the 1994 Criminal Justice and Public Order Act. Crucially, this last contained a number of clauses relating specifically to music which, as Matthew Collin points out in the seminal *Altered State*:

> 'defined and proposed to outlaw – when played in certain circumstances – a genre of music: house. It stated that " 'music' is defined as sounds wholly or predominantly characterised by the emission of a succession of repetitive beats", and for the first time the word "rave" appeared in British legislative language. ... never before ... had a government considered young people's music so subversive as to prohibit it. John Major's government, unlike many pop commentators, obviously didn't consider dance-drug culture to be either meaningless or apolitical'.

And nor should anyone concerned about music censorship today, let alone broader questions of civil rights.

Threats to basic freedoms so often come in the guise of attacks on individuals or works that many don't think worth defending. But in what has come to be known as the 'New Protest' or 'DIY Culture', which is all too often short-sightedly dismissed as 'non-political', music is inextricably bound up with some of the most important political/ideological issues of our time – witness Reclaim the Streets and Exodus. In their most memorable protest RTS dug up a section of motorway using their sound system to cover the noise of hammering drills – those 'repetitive beats' turned against the government once again.

Violinist, Warsaw Ghetto – Credit: Terezin Chamber Music Foundation

Exodus, who feature on our CD, organise not just free parties, but also community training and housing projects; drawing support from local councils and bitter opposition from the police. Far from merely forming a soundtrack to their activities, music is fundamentally interwoven with their radical world-view – the beats drive, unify, identify.

Music has power. As a means of communicating dissent it has few competitors, and it binds as tightly as any other cultural ties. Little wonder then, that music so often draws the censors' fire, even if their assaults eventually prove futile. As the Exodus dub has it 'Babylon them try to ban the beat/but Jah say Exodus we have to/Beat the ban ❏

Julian Petley is a lecturer in media and communication studies at Brunel University

JELLO BIAFRA

Ban Everything

I'm too chickenshit and lazy to think for myself
I want my children to have that comfort too
Just let mail-order religion
Tell me how to raise my kids
But as soon as I let them outside
They come back with all these questions
What's a concerned parent to do?
The answer is obvious –
Ban Everything

I used to laugh at those preachers-for-profit on my TV
When we sat around and watched 'em for yuks
While we were doing all kinds of drugs
The more blasted out of my mind I became,
The more I began to see....
Yes –
There was a void in my life
And Jerry Falwell and Oral Roberts
And Robert Tilton and Pat Buchanan
And – bless his ego – Pat Robertson
Were RIGHT!

The sky is falling!
There's sex on TV
Darwinist *humanism* in the schools
Race mixing in Hollywood
Mighty Mouse promoting drugs
Satanic rock music
Now my children are even being exposed to
Songs written, produced and sung by ... *Negroes*

And each time there was a pre-printed postcard
Where all I had to do was sign my name
And fire it off to my Congressman
And fire it off to the companies
Rev Donald Wildmon told me to tell them I was boycotting
And without even having to write a letter by myself
Or talk to anyone on the phone

Suddenly I had all this *power*
– All this veto power
Power to
Ban Everything

Power to wipe away anything I didn't happen to like
Power to control for others
What I saw no reason to control in my own life
And ya know something?
It felt good
It felt *real* good ...
I was hooked
I was addicted
Yes ... I am a Godaholic

I put my hands on the television screen
I wiggled around my little one-inch prayer cloth
I got in the mail from Robert Tilton
I fondled his holy cornmeal
And a bolt of lightning hit me
– And I got the message

Yo ...
You ain't down with the gang
Till you prove yourself
You gotta start doing favors for the gang
You gotta be the gang's hitmen and hitwimmin
Down at the school board
Down at the shopping malls
(Besides, playing vigilante is your favorite part of the job)
We pick the target
You make the hit
As quietly as possible
There are a lot less of us than they think

We'll start by kneeling together in the den
Smoke a few rocks of ages
When the lynch mob buzz hits
We'll storm out the door
Into the neighborhood
And go *bible wilding!*

Helter Skelter
Domino by domino
We will threaten them
Blackmail their landlords
With picket signs and clinic bombings
Get those books on our blacklist
Out of this here bookstore...
We want every record with a Tipper-sticker
Out of this here record store

Better yet, why don't you close down
And evict those stores altogether
So we can put a nice bible supply store
Or a Blockbuster Video
In their place
Or
We will picket every tenant in your whole shopping mall
And cost you lots and lots of money
Smear your names in the community as vendors of *smut*
Until you see things our way
It's better you just wise up and go along with us
and Ban Everything

We learned about subliminals in Ritz crackers
From the guy who testified at the Judas Priest trial
We learned from an article on Rev. Phil Phillips
And his book, Turmoil in the Toybox
That too much exposure to the Smurfs
Can turn your child into *Charles Manson!*

And we learned from those wholesome comic books
By Chick Publications
That the Pope is the Anti-Christ
And Satan has board of directors meetings in Hell
With drug demons sitting in flaming chairs
Watching episodes of Bewitched
And we learned from the Reverend Joseph Chambers
In Charlotte, North Carolina
That Barney the Dinosaur
Is a New Age *demon*
Who promotes homosexuality!!

I learned from the Daughters of the American Revolution
Why the Diary of Anne Frank
Must be purged from the schools
It's too depressing
And the Secret of Walter Mitty *must go*
Because fantasizing is insanity

I don't want my children exposed
To that lovey-dovey, kissy-kissy, touchy-feely
Smut on TV
Like the Cosby Show
Wholesome violence is the way to go
And I was glad to read
In an Al Menconi religious tract no less
That the most incidents of violence per hour
Were on Pat Robertson's Family Channel network

We went down to Blockbuster and rented *Jaws* last week
And sat down and watched it together in the den
Like a good family should
Next thing I know I sneak a peek at my at my little boy in the bathtub
And he's playing with his rubber shark
In a *funny* way
He's got his fingers in his mouth
And he's movin' it up and down –
No! No! No!
Whap! Whap! Whap!
(Ahh … Latex is good for something)
No! No! No!
Whap! Whap! Whap!
I want my son to grow up
And lead a good life and get a good job
And my daughter to marry well
And churn out lots and lots of grandchildren
Not wander the earth in search
Of mechanical sharks to give them head
The answer is obvious
Ban Everything

Why?
Why?
To protect the children
The little ones

The ones we must shield from any point of view
That might get in the way of our own
And the only way to protect them
From all that adult filth and reality out there
Is to water down and restrict all art
'Till it's safe and easy to understand
For the little children

Because the life of an unborn child is sacred
So once they're born
You can beat 'em
And you can starve 'em
When they turn eighteen send them to the electric chair
Or kill 'em in a war against some starving country
Who had a population explosion
'Cause we cut off their access to birth control
So we'd have someone
To kill
Somewhere
To keep the Pentagon from going broke

So
Ban Everything
Ban Everything
Ban ban ban *Everything!*

Jello Biafra *found himself on trial for obscenity as lead singer of the Dead Kennedys in 1986. Since then he has campaigned for First Amendment rights in the US. He continues to be an activist, a sought-after political and social commentator and he is the founder of Alternative Tentacles Records.* Ban Everything *is reprinted from* Burning Down the Magic Kingdom *to be published April 1 1999 by AK Press (Edinburgh, London, San Francisco). It can be found in recorded form on Biafra's* Beyond the Valley of the Gift Police *(Alternative Tentacles Records, San Francisco).*

CAMILLE PAGLIA

Dissenting sex

EMILY MITCHELL: *What made you interested in writing about Madonna?*

CAMILLE PAGLIA: I immediately loved Madonna's driving, layered disco sound and innovative videos, which combined urban dance-club moves with the avant-garde choreography of Martha Graham. Madonna's overt sensuality and florid glamour revived old Hollywood style at a time when feminism had become drearily over-ideological and anti-fashion. I identified strongly with Madonna as a fellow Italian-American who had similarly come from a close-knit, highly regimented ethnic family and who found Catholic dogma too restrictive.

I first wrote about Madonna in 1990 when the *New York Times* asked me to comment on MTV's brief banning of her video, 'Justify My Love'. An unknown woman called the *Times* after she heard me praise Madonna effusively in a public slide-lecture about images of female sexuality in Hollywood and pop culture. After that, I was constantly asked to talk about Madonna by international media – from England, Holland and Italy to Brazil, Australia and Japan.

Though Madonna has not had her work censored outright in the USA, she has met with censure there and abroad. What characteristics of her work and her public persona do you think drew so much opprobrium?

Madonna deliberately used images of pornography and prostitution to provoke strong reactions not just from political and religious conservatives but from feminists who were then strongly under the influence of anti-pornography polemicists like Catharine MacKinnon and Andrea Dworkin [canonical figures in US women's studies programmes and the authors of Canada's intrusive censorship laws].

You write a good deal in Vamps and Tramps *about the conflicting influence of pagan and Christian elements in western and, in particular, US culture. How*

*do you think that Madonna's use of specifically Christian imagery – like her
video for 'Like a Prayer' which elicited charges of blasphemy from many religious
authorities – situates her in US culture?*

By animating and eroticising a painted statue of a black saint,
Madonna seemed to be zeroing in on the buried, vestigial paganism in
Mediterranean Catholicism that I had studied in my own work. 'Like a
Prayer', however, mixes up Protestant and Catholic iconography in an
unnecessarily confusing way.

Furthermore, by boppily dancing in a skimpy black camisole in front
of a burning cross, Madonna perhaps trivialised and demeaned what is an
atrocious symbol in the USA of anti-black terrorism, arson, and murder
by the Ku Klux Klan. I categorically reject the idea that it was
'censorship' when Madonna lost a lucrative TV commercial sponsored
by Pepsi-Cola which, understandably, refused to give its *imprimatur* to
this video.

For almost a decade, however, Madonna was at the forefront of US
arts and letters in challenging the resurgence of Puritanism among
evangelical Christians, right-wing Republicans, and censorship-minded
feminists, all of whom had conspired to stop *Playboy* and *Penthouse*
magazines from being sold in convenience-store chains.

The repressive coalition of MacKinnonite feminists and religious
conservatives was disastrous for feminism as a progressive movement.
One reason I had tremendous trouble getting published or employed in
the 1970s and 1980s was because my pro-sex wing of feminism (directly
inspired by the 1960s sexual revolution) had been suppressed and
silenced by the feminist establishment. When my controversial book
Sexual Personae was finally published in 1990 (nine years after it had been
completed), it became obvious, I think, how many women throughout
the world agreed with my militant free-speech and pro-porn positions.
We dissidents now have the momentum in feminism, thanks to
Madonna having changed the way millions of young women think about
sexuality.

*Is it the brazen appropriation of old symbols for new uses that makes her
earlier work so exciting? Is it also what offends?*

Yes, Madonna's early and midpoint work was her best because of that first exhilarating burst of aggressive defiance and profanation, in the libertine style of de Sade and Baudelaire. But Madonna's confrontational strategy (through its very success) had become stale by the time of her ill-conceived 1992 book, *Sex*, which may have sold well but was an artistic disaster, banal in design and juvenile in detail. Gimmicky, sadomasochistic scenarios were old hat and, in any case, hardly expressed the health or vitality of the sex impulse – Madonna's ultimate point. After the protracted censorship battle over Robert Mapplethorpe, who had genuinely inhabited the S&M underworld, Madonna's images seemed shallow, superficial, and unerotic.

Madonna has also been adopted as an icon by the gay community. Why do you think this is?

Madonna's disco beat came right out of the gay bar scene. Also, her chameleon-like instinct for costumes and coiffures and her grandiose, diva posturing made her seem more like a drag queen than a normal woman. From her Michigan student days, she was close friends and collaborators with gay men, from whom she got a sense of camp. Her outspoken campaigning for Aids fund-raising later gained the gratitude of gay activists. Finally, she flirted with lesbian innuendoes in several videos and has been rumoured to be bisexual, but her main interests obviously remain men.

What do you think of 'Ray of Light'? How do you think it relates to her other work and to her place as an artist who crosses boundaries?

'Ray of Light' is a very beautiful, contemplative album except for a few moments of self-indulgent mawkishness. However, the idea that this is Madonna's 'best work', as so many people (from Oprah Winfrey on) have claimed, is simply wrong. 'Ray of Light' is rich, high-quality popular music, but from the moment Madonna arrived on the scene in the early 1980s, she was making magnificent music for which she has never been fully honoured by the music industry. Though she has worked with an enormous number of producers, arrangers and co-composers, she always gets the effects she wants. Her signature songs became instant classics, and virtually everything she has done still seems fresh, despite constant airplay.

It's an absurd, post modernist *canard* that Madonna's cultural significance resides entirely in her 'transgressiveness'. Those of us who have loved her work from the start know that some of her most wonderful music – 'Lucky Star', 'Borderline', 'Dress You Up' – is straightforward, empathic, mainstream pop. Ironists never win the world's affection. Madonna is passionate and direct, even when charging down the wrong path.

How do you think the birth of her child has affected Madonna's persona and music? Has it made her more or less transgressive as an artist?

Major artists, from Michelangelo and Beethoven to Picasso, The Beatles and David Bowie, have different stylistic phases. An artist who remains stuck in one mode is generally of a lesser order (which is why it's a good career move to die young, in the full flush of early creativity). It was important that Madonna grow and mature as an artist and as a person – which should have happened before the execrable *Sex* book rather than afterward.

Becoming a mother of course softens a diva's image. It has certainly made Madonna reassess and prioritise, so that she has substituted more tranquil yoga for manic jogging and exercising (which made her too gaunt for my taste).

Having to ponder her child's upbringing and education has made Madonna consider the full implications of her pan-sexual philosophy. The edge is off her Joan of Arc stridency.

Culture too has gradually shifted in the second half of this decade, as the millennium approaches. Through over-repetition and feeble imitation, transgression and subversion have lost their charge everywhere in the art world. We should be concerned now not with defiling and defaming traditional beliefs but in reconstructing, out of the nihilistic ruins left by modernism and post-structuralism, some enlightened new system of affirmative spiritual and political values for the young to embrace. ❏

Camille Paglia *is professor of humanities at the University of the Arts in Philadelphia. She is a culture critic, feminist and libertarian. Her fourth book, a study of Alfred Hitchcock's* The Birds, *was recently released by the British Film Institute. She was interviewed by Emily Mitchell*

MILES MARSHALL LEWIS

Bad as bad can be

'You better swing, batter, batter, swing/'Cause once you get your third felony/Yeah, 50 years you gotta bring/It's a deadly game of baseball/So when they try to pull you over/Shoot 'em in the face, y'all.' ('Deadly Game' C-Bo)

In March 1998, 27-year-old Shawn Thomas, a popular rapper known as C-Bo, was re-jailed in California for a parole violation. Under the terms of a statement handed down from the California Department of Corrections, Thomas had been released on parole in the summer of 1997 with the undertaking that he 'not engage in any behaviour which promotes the gang lifestyle, criminal behavior, and/or violence towards law enforcement'. The nature of his oeuvre, however, dictated that Thomas speak to the realities of ghetto life and street sentiments on US society. Lyrics like 'Deadly Game' from his album 'Til My Casket Drops', returned Thomas to Soledad Prison.

'Rap is a very important and protected form of political expression,' says Elaine Elinson, a lawyer for the American Civil Liberties Union of Northern California. 'It's hard to see the relationship between expressing one's political views and firing a firearm.' (Thomas was originally sentenced to 15 months for firing into the air during a video shoot.) 'Til My Casket Drops' entered the *Billboard* Top 200 chart at number 41, given a boost by the controversies surrounding C-Bo's arrest.

Two days after Thomas's return to prison, prison officials dropped the lyric charge; he remained in prison until August on a lesser violation. After delivering his court statement in the form of a rap, he was released on condition that he record an anti-crime public service announcement.

As the chosen means of expression for young and often disenfranchised African-Americans, hip-hop culture is an obvious magnet for censorship. The case of Shawn Thomas was the most recent and most pointed attack on the free expression inherent in the form but, in 1989, Florida-based Luther Campbell of 2 Live Crew, one of the first succesful rap bands outside the music's home in New York, tested the limits of decency with ribald lyrics delivered over Miami bass beats. Challenged in a case that eventually went to the Supreme Court, 2 Live Crew emerged triumphant from attempts to ban their album 'Nasty As We Wanna Be' on charges of obscenity and indecency. The rap crew celebrated by releasing 'Banned in the USA', the title track sampling Bruce Springsteen's blue collar anthem, 'Born in the USA'.

Death Row Records, whose output had become increasingly popular in the early-1990s, faced action from a surprising quarter. Lobbyist C Delores Tucker, formerly active in the Civil Rights Movement of the 1960s, applied pressure on Death Row's parent label, Interscope Records, and on Time Warner to stop the release of the allegedly obscene album 'Dogg Food' by rap group Tha Dogg Pound.

Tucker did no more than delay the album which finally entered the *Billboard* chart at number one in late-1995, helped to that position by the free publicity supplied by Tucker's campaign. Dogg Pound rappers Kurupt and Dat Nigga Daz likened the subject matter of their rhymes on sexual abuse and gratuitous homicide, to the violence of Hollywood movies. Since movie stars like Arnold Schwarzneggar and Jean-Claude Van Damme were never vilified for the violence of their movies, Tha Dogg Pound reasoned, their own expression deserved the same protection as the popular sceen blockbusters.

In the autumn of 1994, the enterprising, 23-year-old CEO of the fledgling Bad Boy Entertainment, one Sean Combs, hatched a plot to showcase the talents of his rappers Craig Mack and Christopher Wallace of Notorious BIG. Before releasing Wallace's 'Ready to Die' album, 'Puff Daddy' Combs demanded that Wallace excercise a little self-censorship on 'Gimme the Loot' to avoid repercussions that might damage the commerial chances of his new artist.

'Gimme the Loot' is a dialogue between two burglars, a duo so desperate for survival that robbing a pregnant woman is no longer a reprehensible act: 'I don't give a fuck if you're pregnant/Give me the baby rings, and the "number one mom" pendant.' Wallace refused to change his verse and the album, complete with the same style of violence and lewd sexual language as 'Dogg Food', got past the media scrutiny of C Delores Tucker and the censorship watchdogs via a strange

Credit: Redferns

garble on the disk at the strategic moment.

Challenges to complete freedom of expression in hip-hop culture come from many different directions. Though rap music maintains a position at the forefront of the culture, other elements – including graffiti artists and DJs – have also suffered. Spray-painting on subway trains and other available surfaces by aerosol artists throughout New York City was successfully abolished by Mayor Ed Koch in the early 1980s; DJs were badly hit when draconian laws on sampling were introduced in the same decade. Recording companies can now demand such vast sums for the use of samples that classic hip-hop albums such as De La Soul's '3 FeetHigh' and Rising and Public Enemy's seminal 'It Takes a Nation of Millions to Hold Us Back' could not be recorded today.

There are rumours that *Billboard* magazine is about to change the system used to tally their record sales charts by including radio airplay time. Many hip-hop albums top the charts and sell in millions without the benefit of radio exposure, but if the charts system does change, many commercially-minded rap executives may steer their product in the direction of cleaner, less profane, radio-friendly material. ❏

Miles Marshall Lewis is deputy editor of the hip-hop magazine, XXL

JIM D'ENTREMONT

The Devil's disciples

In February 1997, the goth-rock ensemble Marilyn Manson and its eponymous lead singer embarked on a circuit of North American concert venues to promote the album *Anti-Christ Superstar*. As embroidered accounts of the band's performances passed into fact, the disapproval of the pious quickly spiralled into panic. The band's musical stagings were said to incorporate devil worship, live sex, defilement of Bibles, flag desecration, animal slaughter and Grand Guignol effects of indescribably blasphemous obscenity. Circulars produced in Tupelo, Mississippi by the Reverend Donald Wildmon's American Family Association (AFA) warned that Marilyn Manson 'wants to put an end to Christianity through his music.'

Marilyn Manson's pungent fusion of gender-bending and the occult provided a powerful organising and fundraising tool for ideologues whose power base is ignorance infused with fear. Protest demonstrations were assembled in cities throughout the USA by zealots across the sectarian spectrum. Cancellation of a Utah booking triggered a lawsuit. The fundamentalists of Oklahomans for Children and Families tried forcefully but vainly to stop the band from appearing in Oklahoma City. In Indiana, a movement arose to 'bind' the demons of Marilyn Manson through prayer.

When the group joined OzzFest, a concert package headlined by Ozzy Osbourne, the much-reviled former lead singer of Black Sabbath, protests escalated. 'Hate-Rock Rolls Across Country', screamed the *AFA Journal*. In New Jersey, OzzFest had to obtain a legal injunction to honour a performance date; in Virginia, the show was cancelled. Adopting a tactic increasingly popular among Christian activists, the Minnesota Family Council targeted the Minneapolis-based Best Buy

Marilyn Manson – Credit: Mick Hutson/Redferns

Prefiguring theorists of backward-masking and subliminal indoctrination, he insisted that capitalism was being undermined by hidden messages in rock songs. Noebel's findings were supported by Bob Larson's *Rock and Roll: The Devil's Diversion* (1967), which identified the beat of rock as the direct work of Satan. This was the first of a succession of books in which Larson, still active as a lecturer and radio personality, would warn against 'rock's symbiosis with Satanism'.

In the late 1970s, Florida minister Charles Boykin began systematically burning thousands of records, and Steve and Dan Peters of St Paul, Minnesota formed Truth About Rock, an organisation whose inaugural event was a bonfire of musical vanities. The Peters brothers still deliver addresses to schools, youth groups, and evangelical gatherings in which they encourage record-burning. In this period, televangelism was beginning to awaken the political consciousness of Pentecostals and Baptists. Fans of Jerry Falwell's *Old Time Gospel Hour* provided a membership base for the short-lived but iconic Moral Majority; the constituency of Pat Robertson's *700 Club* later became the core of the more durable Christian Coalition. Popular music continues to be a convenient scapegoat for the followers of both Falwell and Robertson.

In 1984, Rick Alley, a Cincinnati businessman incensed by Prince's sexually explicit lyrics, proposed a system of music ratings to help stamp out 'porn rock'. The Recording Industry Association of America (RIAA) ignored this campaign until it was adopted by Tipper Gore, wife of US Vice-President Albert Gore, then a senator from Tennessee. In response to purported obscenities in Prince's *Purple Rain* album, Mrs Gore assembled a coterie of her peers including Christian activist Susan Baker, wife of one of Ronald Reagan's cabinet officials and a national board member of James Dobson's Focus on the Family. Together they formed the Parents Music Resource Center (PMRC) in May 1985. Senate Commerce Committee hearings were convened four months later. Fearing government intervention, the RIAA endorsed a problematic, voluntary, industry-wide system of album-cover advisory labels warning parents of 'explicit lyrics'.

After the fall of communism, right-wing theocrats claimed that Satan was now focused on secular humanist efforts to undermine the US family through abortion, homosexuality, twisted art and sinister music. 'Contemporary music idolises death,' lament Tim and Beverly LaHaye in their book *A Nation Without a Conscience*. In *Learn to Discern*, Bob

Company, sponsor of OzzFest, for a boycott. The AFA urged its 350,000 members to distribute information endorsing the boycott and to ask their friends to take 'Christian action'.

Political analyst Richard Hofstadter notes that in the USA the extreme right has demonstrated 'how much political leverage can be got out of the passions of a small minority'. A network of right-wing authoritarian movements whose alliances are often weak, the theocratic right has far less popular support than it claims to command. Yet it remains one of the most potent antidemocratic forces ever to emerge in the USA. Its adherents are committed to erasing the separation of church and state that is the cornerstone of US democracy. Most of these faith-propelled reactionaries are Protestants – evangelicals, hard-shell Baptists, Pentecostals, members of charismatic sects – united by belief in the unerring literal truth of the Bible, in apocalyptic prophecy, and in justice as clean, swift, merciless and mighty as Jehovah's thunderbolt.

The theocratic right brings true believers into frequently unwitting partnerships with those who know that fear of God's wrath and Satan's guile can be brokered into power and financial gain. Nina Crowley, president of the Massachusetts Music Industry Coalition (Mass MIC), observes that 'while many religious groups may have been founded on lofty moral guidelines, long ago their interest in enlightening society mutated into that of controlling society both morally and politically.' In its pursuit of such ends, the movement is at odds with tenets of free speech articulated in the First Amendment to the US Constitution.

The American political tradition that sanctifies abstract principles of free expression is often at war with its cultural biases in favour of repression. Those biases took root in seventeenth-century Puritan New England and set the tone for the cultural life of colonial America. To most of the American Founding Fathers, art in any form was suspect. A tradition of philistine censoriousness, both religious and secular, has been a constant in US culture.

Beginning in the post-Civil War era, moral crusades led by Anthony Comstock continued into the twentieth century. As soon as jazz began to surface, it was demonised. In August 1921, Anne Shaw Faulkner of the General Federation of Women's Clubs, a bulwark of American Protestantism, published 'Does Jazz Put the Sin in Syncopation?' in the *Ladies Home Journal*. Shaw characterized jazz as 'the accompaniment of the voodoo dancer, stimulating the half-crazed barbarian to the vilest deeds.' By the 1930s, when this uniquely American music had achieved international recognition as an art form, many Americans nonetheless agreed with the Nazi assessment of jazz as *entartete* – decadent – music.

The racism inherent in Faulkner's appraisal of jazz pervaded white attitudes toward rhythm and blues. As a white derivative of black R&B, rock and roll was denounced from the time of its birth in the early 1950s. Southern segregationists like Asa Carter of the North Alabama White Citizens Council complained that rock arose from a Jewish-Marxist plot to drag white youth 'down to the level of the Negro'.

Fear of rock was not confined to Southern bigots. By 1955, 'jungle music' was at the apex of a moral panic over 'juvenile delinquency'. US Senate hearings publicised the virulence of youth-oriented mass media. Clerics of all denominations expressed concern that music was turning American teens into savages. In 1958, the Catholic Youth Center implored its members to destroy whatever records in their possession promoted 'a pagan concept of life'. According to Billy James Hargis's Christian Crusade, rock music was part of a 'systematic plan geared to making a generation of American youth mentally ill and emotionally unstable.'

No amount of alarmist moral rearmament could curb the popularity of Elvis Presley, whose greatest fans belonged to the same Southern white Protestant culture that spawned his most ardent detractors, or of the Beatles, who rode a wave of Anglophilia into worldwide adulation. In 1966, however, when John Lennon imprudently told the *London Evening Standard* that Christianity 'will vanish' and that the Beatles were 'more popular than Jesus now', these statements offended US fundamentalists more vitally than the Beatles' freewheeling attitudes toward sex and drugs. A wave of record-burnings ensued, continuing even after Lennon, fated to be assassinated 14 years later by a born-again Christian, issued an apology.

By 1969, as music began to reflect the general relaxation in censorship, religious anti-rock crusaders could point to a wealth of drug allusions and an increase of profanity. Billy James Hargis's associate David A Noebel, who now heads Summit Ministries in Colorado, was a key proponent of paranoid Christian thinking with regard to music. Author of such diatribes as *Communism, Hypnotism, and the Beatles* (1965), Noebel feared that rock would make 'a generation of American youth useless through nerve-jamming, mental deterioration and retardation.'

Prefiguring theorists of backward–masking and subliminal indoctrination, he insisted that capitalism was being undermined by hidden messages in rock songs. Noebel's findings were supported by Bob Larson's *Rock and Roll: The Devil's Diversion* (1967), which identified the beat of rock as the direct work of Satan. This was the first of a succession of books in which Larson, still active as a lecturer and radio personality, would warn against 'rock's symbiosis with Satanism'.

In the late 1970s, Florida minister Charles Boykin began systematically burning thousands of records, and Steve and Dan Peters of St Paul, Minnesota formed Truth About Rock, an organisation whose inaugural event was a bonfire of musical vanities. The Peters brothers still deliver addresses to schools, youth groups, and evangelical gatherings in which they encourage record–burning. In this period, televangelism was beginning to awaken the political consciousness of Pentecostals and Baptists. Fans of Jerry Falwell's *Old Time Gospel Hour* provided a membership base for the short–lived but iconic Moral Majority; the constituency of Pat Robertson's *700 Club* later became the core of the more durable Christian Coalition. Popular music continues to be a convenient scapegoat for the followers of both Falwell and Robertson.

In 1984, Rick Alley, a Cincinnati businessman incensed by Prince's sexually explicit lyrics, proposed a system of music ratings to help stamp out 'porn rock'. The Recording Industry Association of America (RIAA) ignored this campaign until it was adopted by Tipper Gore, wife of US Vice-President Albert Gore, then a senator from Tennessee. In response to purported obscenities in Prince's *Purple Rain* album, Mrs Gore assembled a coterie of her peers including Christian activist Susan Baker, wife of one of Ronald Reagan's cabinet officials and a national board member of James Dobson's Focus on the Family. Together they formed the Parents Music Resource Center (PMRC) in May 1985. Senate Commerce Committee hearings were convened four months later. Fearing government intervention, the RIAA endorsed a problematic, voluntary, industry-wide system of album-cover advisory labels warning parents of 'explicit lyrics'.

After the fall of communism, right-wing theocrats claimed that Satan was now focused on secular humanist efforts to undermine the US family through abortion, homosexuality, twisted art and sinister music. 'Contemporary music idolises death,' lament Tim and Beverly LaHaye in their book *A Nation Without a Conscience*. In *Learn to Discern*, Bob

DeMoss, youth culture specialist for Focus on the Family, warns of bands who emphasise 'the morbid side of life'. These include AC/DC, Led Zeppelin, Judas Priest, KISS, Motley Crue and Slayer. Christian commentators stress that cult leader Charles Manson was an aspiring musician; serial killer Richard Ramirez was an AC/DC fan; and cannibal Jeffrey Dahmer listened to Iron Maiden. In *Satanism: The Seduction of America's Youth*, Bob Larson cites a young Slayer fan called 'David' who makes pronouncements like: 'I'll murder for the devil. I'm just waiting.'

Characterizing Satan as the personification of totalitarian social control may mask a genuine antipathy toward freedom. In the minds of many, such a powerful authoritarian threat demands authoritarian solutions. Ideologues find in popular music that challenges authority a means of stampeding community leaders, opinion makers, and rank-and-file voters toward authoritarian remedies. The most effective right-wing campaigns exploit real or imagined evidence that the music's content is so far beyond all civilised standards of tolerance that we must dispense with some of our rights in order to vanquish it.

The first right we are asked to jettison is freedom of speech, which in the USA is inconveniently enshrined within the First Amendment. Theocratic organisations attempt to circumvent the First Amendment in five principal ways:

Harassment and intimidation directed at artists in an effort to promote self-censorship These techniques range from anonymous death threats to high-profile lawsuits. In 1985, the parents of a teenage suicide sued Ozzy Osbourne, claiming that his song 'Suicide Solution' drove their son to take his own life. In 1990, the British heavy metal band Judas Priest was sued by parents of another suicide. Although both suits were unsuccessful, they are constantly cited by Christian propagandists seeking to portray the music-suicide link as documented fact.

Prosecution of artists, retail outlets, broadcasters and record companies In 1986 Jello Biafra and the Dead Kennedys were charged under California law for disseminating 'material harmful to minors', ostensibly because their album *Frankenchrist* contained HR Giger's poster 'Penis Landscape'. Biafra was acquitted, but the suit helped facilitate the break-up of the band. In 1990, the rap group 2 Live Crew and a record store owner were prosecuted for obscenity in Florida through the efforts of born-again attorney Jack Thompson. Iran-Contra figure Oliver North later retained Thompson as legal advisor in a drive to induce police departments nationwide to indict seditious musicians. These efforts have had limited success in breaching the wall of First Amendment protections, but their effect is chilling.

Parental advisory labels and ratings Promoted as an alternative to censorship, such systems have historically been tools of the censors. In the recording industry as well as the film industry, artists are often pressured to drop or change material in order to avoid the stigma of age-restricted status. In several states, record dealers have been prosecuted for selling 'stickered' albums to minors. Efforts to proscribe all sales of such albums to persons under 18 have recently been defeated in Wisconsin, Tennessee and Georgia. Legal manouevres in Michigan aimed at applying a ratings system to concerts, while thus far unsuccessful, have won widespread support.

Legislation Apart from labelling and ratings bills, religious activists have pursued such tactics as an 'obscene live conduct' bill in South Dakota. When such unconstitutional state legislation is signed into law, a protracted and expensive legal challenge may be the only means of overturning it. Recent legislative efforts have targeted the corporations that produce and distribute recordings. Last year, Governor George W Bush Jr approved a measure prohibiting the state of Texas or any of its agencies from investing in any private concern that owns at least 10 per cent of any corporation that produces music which 'describes, glamorises, or advocates violence, drug abuse or sexual activity'.

Boycotts. Every issue of the *AFA Journal* contains lists of companies that underwrite the forces Donald Wildmon believes are tearing apart the fabric of society, and offers advice on pressuring them into mending their ways. Triggered by what the AFA calls 'the shameless promotion of homosexuality by Disney/ABC', a boycott of the Walt Disney conglomerate has drawn support from the Catholic League for Religious and Civil Rights, Focus on the Family, the Family Research Council, Concerned Women for America and interdenominational church groups. Disney executives deny that this campaign affects company policy, but early in 1997, shortly after the Southern

Baptist Convention joined the boycott, Disney withdrew Insane Clown Posse's *The Great Milenko*, newly released by its subsidiary Island Records and dubbed 'Satanic' by Christian groups, from stores nationwide. Instances of censorship abound at Disney.

The most effective means of encouraging censorship in a profit-driven industry is economic. The recording industry generates US$12 billion annually. As one corporate entity swallows another, small independent labels have become an endangered species, and artists hold diminished power. In this atmosphere, production and sales executives hasten to avoid offence. Wal-Mart, the largest music retailer in the USA, has responded to pressure campaigns by banning albums with advisory labels from its stores, and successfully insisting that producers and musicians provide the 2300 Wal-Mart outlets with censored versions of their product.

The left might once have gone to battle over such restrictive policies. But the American left has recently retreated from traditional commitments to civil liberties, often aiding right-wing attempts to circumscribe speech. The RIAA has been largely ineffectual in its responses, quick to appease, and willing to live with labels and ratings. 'Our side isn't half as organised as the Christian right,' says Parents for Rock and Rap founder Mary Morello. 'There's too much apathy among believers in free speech. Grassroots organisations of fans and musicians like Mass MIC and the Ohio-based Rock Out Censorship have thus far failed to coalesce into a movement, and lack the massive financial backing that fuels the right.

Mass MIC's Nina Crowley notes that few groups have a more sophisticated understanding of the power of money and how to use it than the theocratic right. 'The success of their new strategies will be determined,' she predicts, 'by whether or not the music industry is willing to sell freedom for profit.' Since under US law a corporation is accorded the same First Amendment rights as an individual, the profit option has the blessings of the Constitution. In a society where corporations control all but a dwindling handful of media outlets, and where public space is being engulfed by privatisation, it is fair to question whether or not the First Amendment still has meaning. ❑

Jim D'Entremont is the head of the Boston Coalition for Freedom of Expression

SUSANA BACA

Out of darkness

The denial of black memory in favour of social assimilation has dogged the Afro-Peruvian experience, burying many of its rhythms

Years ago, somebody at school asked me where my parents were from. I didn't know what to answer. To be black in Peru is not easy. Sometimes it has been painful, often unbearable. At the same time, to be black means to belong to a unique space, a particular way of loving and enjoying.

I was born in Lima and lived in the coastal *barrio* of Chorrillos, where the descendants of slaves have dwelt since the days of the Spanish empire. I am a mixture of a mother who loved dancing and good food and a father who played guitar all the time. Despite good memories, life was not easy during my childhood: people had to work hard. But the good memories are of neighbourhood parties, religious pilgrimages, the military band that played every Sunday after mass.

I am often asked: 'How did you start in music?' I don't believe I ever 'started': music was always part of my world. To be 'in the music' meant belonging to a people whose illusions and happiness were always expressed by the rhythms they inherited as the descendants of slaves brought from Africa to Peru. They expressed confrontation, resistance and assimilation from within.

But the rhythms and cadences through which black families celebrated and dreamed have always lacked wide circulation in Peru. Afro-Peruvian music had no place on the radio nor in record company catalogues when I was a child. Nor were dance venues set aside for it. It was kept alive only in black neighbourhoods, or in households like ours where, while they cooked, my big, cheerful aunts sang with the throaty voices of the black stars of the USA.

I was never told any of this, but I absorbed it while growing up and, in 25 years as a singer, I have had to make a career in a country that did not recognise that black people had contributed anything to its culture. Just a handful of enlightened people believed in the value of Afro-Peruvian music, notably Don Porfirio Vasquez and Nicomedes Santa Cruz. For years I followed their example.

In Spanish, *recuperar* means to recover the past, to rescue it from the ravages of time. It also means to shepherd together that which has drifted apart, carrying the additional, if more obvious, meaning of recovery, healing, getting better.

I searched for, and gathered songs and fragments, recovering styles that were long believed lost: the *festejo*, a song and dance tradition of ecstatic happiness; the *zamacueca*, sultry music danced late at night; the *landó* that marries both rural and urban sensuality; the *panalivio* and other religious songs used in times of pilgrimage. I remembered the lonely *coplas* and the *cumananas*, the older ways of singing and making poetry. Like Afro-Peruvian culture itself, they are mixtures of very different forms and themes. With them I celebrate a culture that is alive from its roots.

Over the past 20 years, there has been increasing recognition of the black contribution to music. This reassessment has a lot to do with the boom in tropical rhythms promoted by the music industry which, in turn, has led to a greater africanisation of music and dance. But it would be quite misleading to confuse this phenomenon with the emotions which triggered its original musical expression.

It took me some time to discover that black Peruvians had themselves decided it was better to forget their terrible times as slaves. They succeeded so well they ended up by truly forgetting. As a result, many melodies have been lost forever, along with the singing and performing styles and even the skill of making the old instruments.

I believe that identity must be reasserted and redefined for our era on new foundations dug into the solidity of tradition. I live my musical life as part of the permanent process of recreating tradition. Because within me, I know, is a part of the Afro-Peruvian memory. ❏

Susana Baca is co-founder with her husband of the Instituto Negrocontinuo (Black Continuum) in Lima. Her latest CD, 'Susana Baca', is released by Luaka Bop

GERALD SELIGMAN

It will pass

Throughout the years of Brazilian dictatorship [1964-1985], Chico Buarque was an eloquent and accomplished critic whose songs were cherished and memorised even as they were banned. As his opposition and influence grew, he became more of a threat. During one of his concerts, during which he shared the stage with Gilberto Gil, military censors actually forbade them to sing. So they hummed and whistled and the entire audience sang the lyrics in their stead. Exile soon followed: Chico to Italy, Gil and his friend Caetano Veloso to England.

Soon after returning from exile, Chico Buarque resumed his role as critic in song. Much to the delight and surprise of the country and probably the result of a lapse in official vigilance at carnival time, one song, *Vai Passar* (It Will Pass), actually escaped the censors for a few short weeks. There on the radio was an ebullient samba, purportedly a celebration of carnival, but actually celebrating the day when the dictatorship would end and the 'banner of its madness' would pass. It wasn't long before the authorities caught on and *Vai Passar* went the same way as most of Buarque's music. ❏

Gerald Seligman, *a specialist in world music, works for EMI*

Vai Passar

(Music: Francis Hime/Chico Buarque; Lyric: Chico Buarque)

It will pass
On the avenue, a popular samba
Each cobblestone
Of the old city
Tonight will shudder
To remember
That here immortal sambas have
passed
That here through our bloody feet
Here we danced samba with our
ancestors

In time
This sad page of our history
This yellowed passage in the
memory
Of our newer generations
Will sleep
Our mother country so distracted
Without noticing what was taken
In tenebrous transactions
Its children
Roaming blindly through the
continent
Who dragged stones like penitents
Building strange cathedrals

And one day, at last
They'd have the right to a fleeting
happiness
The panting epidemic
That we call carnival
O carnival, o carnival

(It will pass)

Applaud for the wing[1] of the
famished barons
The block[2] of the re-dyed
Napoleons
And the pygmy Bolivars
My God, come look
Come see right here a city singing
The evolution of liberty
Until the break of day

Ah, what a good life, oleré[3]
Ah, what a good life, olerá
The banner[4] of madness will pass
Ah, what a good life, oleré
Ah, what a good life, olerá
The banner of madness
Will pass. ❏

Translated by Gerald Seligman

1 Carnival parades are made up of different wings within the one
parade, with each wing in different costume, in this case, dressed
as faded royalty and military
2 A block (bloco) is a larger carnival group
3 Oleré, Olerá are Gods in Candomblé, the syncretist religion of
the Brazilian people.
4 Carnival paraders customarily carry banners representing their
samba schools, as the groups are called.

YEVGENY YEVTUSHENKO

Fears

Fears are dying out in Russia,
like the wraiths of bygone years;
only in church porches, like old women,
here and there they still beg for bread.
I remember when they were powerful and mighty
at the court of the lie triumphant.
Fears slithered everywhere, like shadows,
penetrating every floor.
They stealthily subdued people
and branded their mark on everyone:
when we should have kept silent they taught us to scream,
and to keep silent when we should have screamed.
All this seems remote today.
It is even strange to remember now.
The secret fear of an anonymous denunciation,
the secret fear of a knock at the door.
Yes, and the fear of speaking to foreigners?
...
I see new fears dawning:
the fear of being untrue to one's country,
the fear of dishonestly debasing ideas
which are self-evident truths;
the fear of boasting oneself into a stupor,
the fear of parroting someone else's worlds,
the fear of humiliating others with distrust
and of trusting oneself overmuch.
Fears are dying out in Russia.
And while I am writing these lines,
at times unintentionally hurrying, I write haunted by the single fear
of not writing with all my strength.

Lyric used by Shostakovich in Symphony Thirteen – 'Babi Yar'

MSTISLAV ROSTROPOVICH

Out from under

The cellist, pianist and conductor Mstislav Leopoldovich Rostropovich, was born on 27 March 1927 in Baku, Azerbaijan. He joined the Moscow Conservatory in 1943 where he studied composition with Dmitry Shostakovich and won the gold medal in the first All-Soviet Music Competition at the age of 18. In 1951, he won the Stalin Prize and five years later was appointed professor of cello at the Moscow Conservatory. With his wife Galina Vishnevskaya, a leading soprano with the Bolshoi, he became one of the first Soviet 'ambassadors of culture' and made regular concert tours to the West in the 1950s and 60s. His troubles with the authorities began in 1970 when he wrote an open letter to the Soviet press in support of Alexander Solzhenitsyn who had just been expelled from the Writers' Union after winning the Nobel Prize. The letter was never published within the USSR; Rostropovich and Vishnevskaya were banned from foreign travel for four years

Rostropovich and Vishnevskaya were given permission to leave the Soviet Union in 1974; in 1978, they were stripped of their Soviet citizenship. Attempts were made to erase all record of their contribution to Soviet music: photographs of Vishnevskaya vanished from the Bolshoi archive; Rostropovich's name was removed from the dedication page of Shostakovich's Cello Concerto which he had premiered in 1959. It was not until 1990, after the fall of the Berlin Wall, that Rostropovich returned to Russia as musical director of the National Symphony Orchestra, Washington, DC.

In January 1975, the Russian nationalist writer Igor Shafarevich

published a piece in the émigré magazine *Russkaya Mysl*. 'O *sbornike iz-
pod glyb*' (On the collection 'From under the rubble') attacked the latest
wave of Soviet emigration to the West. 'The most representative figures
from Soviet literature, criticism and culture left the country of their own
free will,' he wrote. 'Some say they were forced into exile, others that
they were all but forced out, others still that they have been deprived of
their citizenship. This suggests that they have all failed to act as they
should.' In March the same year, Rostropovich responded to
Shafarevich's attack in an open letter to the magazine:

> I was a musician, never a politician. I lived according to the
> dictates of my conscience and my heart. I did not sign letters put
> together by official agencies, whether against 'Israeli aggressors',
> Pasternak or Sakharov. I never participated in poisonous official
> campaigns against composers, writers, artists, scientists and, as is
> well known, I gave refuge to my friend Aleksandr Solzhenitsyn in
> my country house, where he spent four winters. These 'crimes'
> carried a trail of consequences in their wake; as a result I left
> Russia with my family. ...
>
> Igor Shafarevich writes 'they left of their own free will'. What
> does 'of their own free will' mean, exactly? How does Igor
> Rostislavovich Shafarevich imagine my creative life at home, as an
> artist deprived of any means of self-expression? What is to be
> done when a performer's art is aging and dying with him? The
> only tangible mark that a musical performance can make is a
> recording that might outlive the performer (though even this is
> inadequate). But you need permission to record, at least. And
> what if an official's whim scuppers a recording in full flow and you
> are effectively hounded out of the studio - as happened to my
> wife, Galina Vishnevskaya, during a recording of Puccini's *Tosca*,
> to myself as conductor and to the Bolshoi Theatre orchestra?
>
> How long am I supposed to endure being treated like a puppet
> whenever I plan my foreign tours? I am entirely in the hands of
> the state agency *Goskontsert* which trades in musicians. Only it can
> say where I may or may not go, what I can and cannot play. And
> everything depends on its - or somebody's - arbitrary wish. Why
> is it that when they don't want to allow me to go to Paris to play
> the Beethoven Trio with Yehudi Menuhin and Wilhelm Kempff
> (at the Ionesco Jubilee Concerts in January 1974), they send an

official telegram to Yehudi Menuhin saying that I can't travel because I am ill, when in fact I am perfectly well?

How many plans can they ruin, how long will I have to be 'in quarantine' and how many foreign tours and concerts can they cancel? ...

I am still 47, I'm at the height of my powers. There is so much I could do for my country if only they would give me my 'musical freedom' without 'cutting me down to size', without 'tripping me up', ruining my plans, without trying to destroy me as a person and as a musician, just to prove that a talented personality can be broken too if he misbehaves, and that a mediocrity can be put in his place - the sort who will submit to the authorities without question and toe the narrow and often fatuous official line blindfold.

There is so much suspicion, so much control and such a desire to play safe. I made hundreds of plans, I dreamt of conducting Shostakovich's opera *Katerina Izmailova* and all his symphonies; Tchaikovsky's *Queen of Spades*, Musorgsky's *Boris Godunov* ... When I was hounded out of the Bolshoi theatre I didn't stop: I made arrangements for a performance of the *Queen of Spades* with the Tashkent Opera and a group of performers came over to Moscow for preliminary discussions. I also talked about the *Queen of Spades* with the Baku Opera, and about a new production of *Prince Igor* in Vilnius. But for the umpteenth time it was all forbidden. I was even removed from the Moscow Operetta a week before the proposed premiere of Johann Strauss's *Die Fledermaus*, on which I had worked without payment for months. ...

Physically, one can bear almost anything. My wife survived the siege of Leningrad. With our people we have lived through all the torment, the hunger, the pain of war. But this is possible only when there is a chance of fulfilling one's dream in the future. A musician cannot stay walled in and work for himself alone. He has to return his art to others; with no outlet, art kills the artist.

My wife and I have left not our people, but the officials who have been given the opportunity to make a mockery of those who have devoted their lives to art. We did not leave because we did not have enough love at home, or recognition, comfort or money. On the contrary, our life abroad is much harder. Our children are living in a Swiss guest-house; we are constantly moving from city to city, living in hotels for a few days at a time, without the comforts we had at home in our beautiful flat and our enormous *dacha*. We left only to fulfil our musical aspirations. Vegetation, the mere preservation of life for its own sake, cannot be the lot of those with any capacity to be truly creative. ❏

From an Open Letter from **Mstislav Rostropovich** *to the émigré paper* Russkaya Mysl, *13 March 1975* *Translated by Irena Maryniak*

MEXICO

Songs at the factory gates
Dolores Cortéz

Singer-songwriter León Chaves Texeiro is a victim of one of the most effective forms of censorship - exclusion. Though he has released three albums and some of his songs have achieved the status of workers' anthems in Mexico, he has always been left out of the mainstream. 'I don't mind being excluded,' he said. 'I go to the factories and working fields and I play there.'

Only once has he appeared on television. In 1987, a director friend with a state-run channel invited him onto the programme *Metropolis*. Against his better interests, Chaves sang one of his most polemical songs. The programme was subsequently banned - though not before the song had been re-edited with the words 'police' and 'assassination' removed. On 2 October Mexico mourned the 30th anniversary of Tlatelolco massacre in which 300 students were killed in demonstrations at the Olympic Games. 'I sing for those people that were shot for expressing their views,' said Chaves, whose lyrics describe the gritty lives of Mexico's burgeoning poor.

FLEMMING ROSE

Rock the Kremlin

It was the summer of 1996 and the eve of presidential elections.
Former secretary general of the Communist Party and one-time
President of the Soviet Union Mikhail Gorbachev was campaigning in St
Petersburg in the hope of securing a return to the Kremlin.

In an attempt to woo younger voters, Gorbachev paid a visit to the
grave of Viktor Tsoi, the rock poet who had died in a car accident in
1990 aged 28. At the time of his death, Gorbachev knew next to
nothing about the rock poet and his legendary group *Kino*, part of the
despised and persecuted Soviet rock-culture. Now Tsoi was an icon of
the new Russia, and the once all-powerful head of state needed a photo-
op in the shadow of his grave. The times had changed indeed.

As with so much on the Russian cultural scene, rock'n'roll arrived
from the West in the 1960s and the Beatles were to blame. Most groups
in the first wave of Soviet rock cited the Beatles as their main influence
and inspiration. However, legend has it that it was the Rolling Stones
who scared the hell out off the minister of culture, Valentina Furtseva,
when she or one of her aides attended a Stones concert in Warsaw in
1967. 'We're not having anything like that in our country,' she
supposedly said.

True or not, the Soviet authorities fought for control of rock culture
as soon as they became aware of it. Contrary to their western peers, the
Soviet rock bands and their audiences did not long for 'satisfaction',
merely artistic independence. There were few if any references to sex in
Soviet rock lyrics, nor did they engage in anti-war rhetoric against
Soviet military involvement around the globe. They did not oppose the
invasion of Afghanistan in 1979, or speak out against racism or
communist ideology. At least not openly.

The Soviet rock scene wanted only to put its existential problems
into words and rhythm. But even that turned out to be too

revolutionary in a society where any activity outside the domain of the state, be it a club of stamp collectors or young people playing rock'n'roll, was looked on as a political challenge to the Party.

'In our country the call for freedom sounded in a totally different situation,' says Russian rock critic Artyom Troitsky. 'In all spheres of life the individual was subject to oppression and violence. The total lack of freedom and the total lack of truth: those were the issues keeping our minds busy in the first booming years of Soviet rock. And those issues are at the centrepiece of the story about Soviet rock.'

And it was the lyrics, not the beat, he adds, that were the driving force of Soviet rock. 'In this country it has always been more important and dangerous to speak out. Rock music has always flirted with danger.' It immediately became part of the same counter-culture that ran through all forms of artistic expression in the totalitarian state. As with literature for a different audience, for youth rock became the mouthpiece and forum of free and open debate.

Rock artist were subject to the same kind of persecutions as writers, journalists and painters who did not want to sign up for the official ideological line. Andrei Romanov, leader of the group *Voskresenie* (Resurrection) was jailed in the early 1980s; Jury Shvechuk and his group DDT had to flee the provincial town of Ufa and move to Leningrad because the local authorities were out to get them.

In mid-1983, the ministry of culture decreed that the repertoire of any rock group must include at least 80 per cent of songs written by members of the Union of Composers – by the official musical establishment. None of the groups on the Soviet rock scene had membership in that exclusive club, and the move was clearly intended to make their lives more difficult.

A decree issued by the ministry of culture in the summer of 1984 banned the performance in public of 41 Soviet bands, among them *Bravo, Centr, Akvarium, Kino*, DDT and Nautilus Pompilius, on account of 'a growing interest for Soviet rock groups among foreign tourists.' It also called for a ban on 34 western artists from Julio Iglesias to Iron Maiden, as well as Pink Floyd's album 'The Final Cut'(1983), in which the line 'Brezhnev took Afghanistan/Begin took Beirut/Galtieri took the Union Jack' gave the minister a serious headache. A ban 'in Moscow on music that depicts our life in a distorted way and makes propaganda for ideals and attitudes alien to our society' followed.

The arrival of *glasnost* in 1987 turned Soviet reality upside down; rock culture became an integral part of official culture. The most famous bands were invited to perform on television and their records were sold by the million. With the demise of the Soviet state in 1991, the transition to a market economy and the creation of a private domain outside the reach and control of the state, the rock scene gained total freedom.

Its victory was not without ambivalence. 'In many ways rock gained from the process of democratisation,' says Troitsky, 'but in others it lost: it lost its monopoly. Rock used to be one of very few reservations where an animal by the name 'truth' could walk around. Now the creature ranged all over society. And many of the new press publications turned out to be smarter, deeper and sharper than the childish revelations by our rock-artists.'

Slava Butusov, songwriter, guitarist and singer in Nautilus Pompilus, one of the most popular bands in the 1980s, compares the situation before and after the fall of the censor-state. 'I don't want to say it was a good time in the old days. It was a grey and awful time, but in a way it was easier. Anybody who had the courage to go on stage and sing a few critical words was celebrated as a member of the most sophisticated avant-garde. Nobody asked questions about artistic expression, form and content, if only you said something critical.'

'Today you are judged by your individual professionalism. It's like stepping out into a open field, where you have the freedom to move in any direction. That's very difficult. If somebody puts up road signs with prohibitions it's easy; you just have to find a way round the signs to move forward. But from an artistic and existential point of view the most difficult thing is to end up in an open space, where you have to make your own choices without any interference from outside.' ❑

Flemming Rose was Moscow correspondent of the Danish newspaper Berlingske Tidende *(1990-1996). He is the author of* The catastrophe that didn't happen: Russia in transition 1992-1996 *(Gyldendal, Copenhagen 1997)*

GERARD MCBURNEY

Surviving Stalin

The story of Dmitri Shostakovich *is* the story of Soviet music, official and unofficial. His life dominates the whole central arch of this story, from his eruption onto the world stage with his First Symphony in 1926, through Stalin's repression of the mid-30s to the renewed onslaught on composers following World War II and, in the end, through to Kruschev and Brezhnev

At first sight, the history of Soviet music appears to divide sharply between the official and unofficial. In fact, things were far more chaotic and fragmented, with musicians of vastly different talents and ideology flirting with both sides and things sometimes changing even from month to month, depending who was in charge. Though there was no lack of confrontation, the relationship was symbiotic rather than confrontational. One of the things that today embitters composers who went through all that is the revelation that their supposedly unofficial art was almost parasitic on the official music it purported to oppose.

The Soviets, like so many others, have always been great rewriters of history. For instance, both Stalinist and post-Stalinist rewriting of history encouraged a vastly oversimplified view of the situation before 1932 and the organisation of the arts unions. They characterised it as a straight struggle between the proletarian movements represented principally by RAPM (Russian Association of Proletariat Musicians) and the so-called ASAM (Association of Contemporary Music), supposedly the haven for the real artists, both the old-fashioned kind like Miaskovsky, inheritors of the Rimsky, Tchaikovsky mantle, and the out and out modernists like the young Shostakovich. Although the truth is more complicated, there's no doubt that the proletarian organisations and RAPM posed a serious threat to people's livelihoods.

The early 1930s sees the unionisation of the arts world. Art must be organised, brought under the rubric of propaganda and coopted for the so-called education of the people in something called social realism.

In the midst of all this, something extraordinary happens. Around 1926, the child prodigy Dmitri Shostakovich bursts on the scene. At the age of 20, he takes the world by storm with his First Symphony, written as a graduation exercise for the Leningrad conservatoire where he had been a child pupil. Within a few months of its appearance it has been performed hundreds of times all over the world. In one step he had become one of the most famous composers in the world, a position he retained for the rest of his on the whole fairly unhappy life.

This presented the Soviets with a problem: Shostakovich had become a much-sought-after cultural phenomenon abroad. The foreign press wrote about him and this was worrying. Remember, during this whole period the three most famous living Russian composers - Prokofiev, Stravinsky and Rachmaninov - are all living abroad. Now, suddenly, here was a boy already famous in the West and, understandably, there was an urge to say: 'Look what our Soviet cultural system can produce: it produces geniuses.' You in the West no longer have Beethovens, only decadents like Schoenberg and Stravinsky. Here we have Shostakovich.' But there's a worry because it's clear this art is difficult, not 'proletarian'.

For a while things go along reasonably enough; Shostakovich's Second and Third Symphonies, the October Symphony and the First of May Symphony, were written for famous revolutionary celebrations – the tenth anniversary of the October revolution in1927 and the May Day celebrations of 1928. In each case, they have slogan-like choruses at the end in a wild, whacky style and are written in very bold, very hyper, very avant-garde language, brightly coloured, at once abstract and bizarrely 'concrete'.

The symphonies were a mixed success, though Shostakovich himself seems to have seen them as a compromise and was later angry with himself for having written in this way. Most of his time at this period was spent in the theatre, the cinema the music hall, the ballet. He wrote a number of film scores, for silent films and then for the talkies. He wrote for political theatre, he wrote for avant-garde Shakespeare productions He even worked with Vsevolod Meyerhold, Alexander Rodchenko and Vladimir Mayakovsky on the first production of the latter's *Bedbug*. He's still a boy, but he's swimming in this world of stars; he's one of the stars.

Shostakovich at the piano, Mayakovsky (standing), Meyerhold (seated) and Rodchenko discussing Shostakovich's music for Mayakovsky's Bedbug *– Credit: Lebrecht Collection*

And suddenly they are all gone: almost every one of these people ends badly. Moreover, the political temperature is mounting and Shostakovich's overnight success in the West had made him enemies at home. There's naturally resentment and jealousy of him among less talented composers and these begin to play the political game. The politics of art in the Soviet Union is riddled with envy. Although he is well aware of all this, Shostakovich does little to endear himself. When he thinks what what others are doing is absurd, he scarcely conceals his scorn and, inevitably, lays up some of his future troubles.

After writing his early avant-garde masterpiece *The Nose* (based on a Gogol story), Shostakovich wanted to write a full length opera. With his librettists, he rejigged a short story by Leskov in a way that has been the subject of passionate debate ever since.

When you talk about music and text you are always in trouble. If the music is any good at all, there is a tension between the music and the words. Discussions of the text of *Lady Macbeth of the Mtsensk District* tend to ignore its structure as a drama, treat it as a political text. Whether or not the changed status of its heroine Katerina is politically motivated, it is definitely dramatically motivated; certainly in terms of the time, you couldn't make a story like that stand up in the theatre without the audience being drawn to a classical or sentimental heroine.

At any rate, *Lady Macbeth* represents the young composer stepping out. Though the avant-garde language is still there in chunks, it is subsumed into a much broader, more urgent, film-music-like populist language designed to knock them flat in the back row of the ninepennies. It shows Shostakovich moving out from one relatively contained and clear area of operation, the avant-garde, but not transferring himself into another one, the writer of patriotic tunes or whatever. Instead, he's moved into an open area where it's hard to control him.

Moreover, in the first two acts, the piece has two scenes of stunning violence, one of which is the gang assault of a peasant woman. In the other, Sergei, the leader of the assault on the peasant woman, turns up in the heroine's room in the middle of the night and seduces her, a rape too, in a way, but quite different. Dramatically, he releases in Katerina, the heroine, a colossal erotic charge. She is bored with her stifling marriage, impotent husband and lustful father-in-law. She discovers what she really wants from this rough foreman, who says he's come to borrow a book.

And the music of this notorious passage is the music of climax: they have a duet of encounter – you can hardly call it a love duet – where the act of copulation is described in the most graphic way by the orchestra. The staging demands a huge bed. This was called pornography, but it's not; it's almost comedy, it's satire because what comes across is not the erotic charge you get from *Tristan and Isolde*, it's a sort of Gogolian mockery of the animal, the hollow laughter of humans as animals.

And the disaster came when Stalin got up with his cronies and walked out of the box. Some days later, Shostakovich, who was on tour playing in the north, got a telegram from friends saying buy the newspaper and on page three of *Pravda,* some say written by Stalin himself, he found the infamous article 'Muddle instead of Music'. This legendary moment was unlike any other in the history of European music that I can think of.

And it launched a vicious campaign against Shostakovich. He returns to Leningrad and people cross the street to avoid him; his ballet *The Bright Stream* – a straight piece of early Stalinist tat – which has run for some months already at the Bolshoi, is suddenly denounced as 'balletic falsehood' and taken off. He is described as a lacky, a toady of the West, a bourgeois composer, a man personally seeking to undermine socialism. The Fourth Symphony, one of his most extraordinary and abrasive scores, a huge work, was stopped in the middle of rehearsal in May the same year. It was a quarter of a century before he heard it again.

This single episode seems to have changed his life: it turned him into another kind of human being. Almost within the space of a few days, this brilliant boy, this wit, this savage ironist turned into another lind of artist altogether, the composer we now think of as the dark tragedian of the mid-twentieth century. For example, the language of the quartets comes out of this episode. Before this period there's no 'abstract' music at all, it's nearly all theatre music, all drama, all parody.

From being a golden boy, he became a measure of the regime's desire to control artists. The official structures of Soviet musical life are galvanized to devour the man who is their king, their prize, their centre, their main export. It hardly seems an accident that Prokoviev is finally persuaded to return at this point. You could say his return fits into a completely different pattern: the return of Gorky and, in a different way, the return of Eisenstein; the assiduous courting of the men who have gone to the West whom the authorities would love to have home again. They even tried with Diagilev but to no effect.

In the end, they destroyed Eisenstein, they destroyed Gorky and, finally, they destroyed Prokofiev.

So, throughout 1935, 1936, 1937, you have the clearly intentional destruction, persecution and public shaming of this central figure, Shostakovich, who was virtually unperformed by that stage; on the other side of the same coin, you have an older 'great' composer who is persuaded to return and be the new king, only to find, as Shostakovich reportedly put it later, that 'he had fallen like a chicken into the soup'.

Meanwhile, Shostakovich, who seems to have considered all kinds of solutions to the situation, suddenly produces the Fifth Symphony. It was a tumultuous success. He had changed his language completely; for many this was a shock. There are those who believe the symphony to be the creation of a new musical language of double-speak that 'fully expresses the tragedy': that when people first heard it, they understood it to be the appearance of a musical language that, unlike literature or painting, would be clear without being censored in the face of the purges then in full sway. But there are those who thought that it was quite the opposite: a gross reversion to a conservative, essentially corny and reactionary idiom, grossly dependent on film music and on the music of the past.

I refuse to believe that the issues can so easily be reduced. The pressures that produce a musical language are far more subtle; they exist at a level of eruption. And, one thing was clear: Shostakovich was under such pressure as a human being that he was reborn as an artist with a new language. It's extraordinary that this same period should have produced the Fifth as well as Prokoviev's nice little propaganda piece, Peter and the Wolf, both born out of an extremely ugly situation.

The Fifth turned him back into a hero, but of a new kind. It made him the hero of the intelligentsia, which he hadn't been before. The 1937 first performance of the Fifth seems now to have been a defining moment for the place of serious music in the endless moral debate that went on for so long among the Soviet intelligentsia. People who were at the Leningrad premiere tell you that so many people were in tears, even intellectuals. Even Ehrenburg felt this was a work that voiced a predicament. And more: it is in music's power to give dignity, sentimental dignity to a situation. Notwithstanding the fact that to many western musicians who heard this music it seemed precisely to be lacking in dignity, for those who heard it in context, it dignified their situation. Outside that context, its presumptions seemed false.

At the same time, the same piece did all the things that Soviet composers were being asked to do – write in a more conservative language, an official musical language – and it restored him to some kind of official favour. With the Fifth Symphony, we arrive at one of the central problems affecting all talented composers, even Prokofiev, as well as Shostakovich. For the next 20 years, like so many other artists until the death of Stalin, these men were to go up and down, up and down; they were treated like yo-yos. And I return to the idea of envy, to the festering politics of the Union of Composers. Prokoviev and Shostakovich were constantly being accused of letting down the Soviet people, of failing to write the music that the Soviet people needed. Yet the ideological demands made on them were, from their very conception, incoherent. Like the demands of critics in the West, or schoolteachers, or audience votes, they are dependent on a fundamental misunderstanding of the nature of the artistic enterprise.

The moment you attempt to control style, the moment you confuse style and content, you fall into a morass which is as old as the hills. People are still tearing each other apart over the Fifth: some say the ending is what the Soviet authorities said it was – a tub-thumping affirmation of the victory of the Soviet ideology – others that it's what the intelligentsia at the time felt – a hollow, disastrous, tragic, grief-stricken depiction of the human soul being crushed under the weight of Stalinism. But it could be both at exactly the same time.

It's the ambiguity, even more, the ambivalence of this music tht is its shifting centre. The ambivalence is disturbing. All sorts of people want to claim this man for their own and everywhere they move, he shifts his ground, either to join them or undermine them.

Then comes World War II and Shostakovich writes another blockbuster in the form of the Leningrad Symphony. It was supposedly smuggled out on microfilm on a convoy. Russia was now the ally and this music became a huge piece of Allied propaganda, performed endlessly on US radio. Shostakovich appeared famously on the cover of *Time* magazine, wearing a fireman's helmet. These images are too hard to

Shostakovich firefighting on the roof of the Leningrad Conservatoire, 1941 – Credit: Lebrecht Collection

shake off. By the end of the war, Shostakovich is identified in the minds of the even mildly culturally aware world outside the Soviet Union with the aspirations of the Soviet people. Even the briefest perusal of the music with open ears tells you that simply doesn't work, but it colours the way he's been seen ever since. Yet at the same time, that's not to say this piece can simply be reinterpreted a a piece of anti-Soviet propaganda: interpretation is something done by the listener, not the composer.

It's curious tht after World War II, Shostakovich becomes, in spite of himself, the most 'official' of official composers – except that all the official composers around him continue to hate him, resent his success

and seek to undermine him more and more, largely because of the sheer
scale of his talent. In 1946 and 1947, you have renewed attacks on
writers and film makers, followed in 1948 by Zhdanov's attack on the
Union of Composers. Musical conservatives such as Vladimir Zakharov,
Tikhon Khrennikov and Ivan Dzerzhinsky back his onslaught on
Shostakovich, along with Prokofiev, Khachaturian, Miaskovsky – who is
very old by now – Shebalin and Popov, an interesting composer who
took refuge in drink. Shostakovich is pilloried as an enemy of the
people. This was a second devastating public humiliation.

Then comes the thaw under Kruschev; Shostakovich is perched,
uncomfortably, between a large number of different worlds. He's already
writing a musical comedy and tries his hand at pop songs, or *estrada*
songs. He wrote a hilarious, sugary number, 'The Motherland Hears',
which, we're told, Gagarin sang on his first trip into space and broadcast
back to the expectant world. It was a genuinely popular song and not a
bad tune.

From the mid-1950s, he is under gathering pressure to join the
Communist Party which, to the disillusionment of his friends and the
younger generation, he finally did in 1961. After 1936 and 1948, it was
the third of the landmarks that scar his life. By this time, Shostakovich is
older, he is ill and his self-respect took a colossal dive.

He survived until 1975 by which time the post-Stalin generation of
composers had emerged – Schnittke, Gubaidulina, Denisov, Pärt
Hrabovsky and others – many of whom he knew and protected in one
way or another. They became part and parcel of what was called
'alternative', 'unofficial', 'leftist' 'modernist' 'westernising' 'avant-garde'
and their music was little performed at home despite being their being
patted on the head abroad. Perhaps they made him feel isolated as an
artist, even out of touch with the language of modern music. Late public
works like the Thirteenth Symphony – the Babi Yar Symphony that uses
Yevtushenko poems and had trouble with the censors – or the
Fourteenth Symphony, do seem in part to be attempts to appeal
especially to the conscience of the younger generation. Then again,
perhaps Shostakovich was simply trying to restore a sense of his own
worth.

By this stage, he is publicly treated as a great elderly genius – but
there's no doubt he was lonely. Certainly the private chamber music he
is writing is music of intense solitude. And there I go again,

60   INDEX ON CENSORSHIP 6 1998

'interpreting' this music.

It's a difficult and complex story and it's a story that is rewritten every day. I said earlier that the Soviets are obsessed with rewriting their own history. Around 1989, when everything is starting to fall apart, secretaries from the Musicians' Union – the very people who had pilloried him – start repenting in public and jumping on the 'revision' of Shostakovich's reputation. They talk of him as a saint, literally. He becomes the 'Piman of our times'; the saintly monk in Boris Gudonov who writes the chronicle of the age in which, he says, he is secretly writing down the true history of Russia so that future generations shall know the truth about the brutally of the Tsars. It was revolting.

When you hear the battles, couched as they so often are in fashionable terms, about how we should 'read' this music, I long for the day we no longer have to read it, but just listen to it.

At the height of his powers, this man produced works that moved people intensely. Within that society they held out a hand to those who wanted to listen. For those who needed that experience, they dignified a terrible waste of life, a senseless, pointless waste of time. Perhaps that's even truer now – and why the controversy surrounding his work continues so passionately.

Of course, there were and still are, especially in our own culture, serious musicians who hated his music for so long because it sounds 'cheap', like a film track. Well of course it is; that's its whole point. ❏

Gerard McBurney talking with Judith Vidal-Hall. He is a composer, broadcaster and teacher at the Royal Academy of Music, London

VLADIMIR ASHKENAZI

Broken rhythm

The celebrated Russian pianist and conductor, Vladimir Ashkenazi, was born in Gorky in 1937 and made his debut as a pianist at the age of seven. he studied at the Central Music School in Moscow and at the Moscow Conservatoire. After winning many international prizes, he defected to the UK in 1963. From 1978-1996, he was musical director of the Royal Philharmonic Orchestra and now conducts the Czech Philharmonic Orchestra. He has lived in Iceland since 1972

IRENA MARYNIAK *What did it mean to be a musician in the Soviet Union in the 1950s and 60s?*

VLADIMIR ASHKENAZI In terms of musical education – the teachers you had and the students you met – life was intensely interesting. Music was well placed because it was so generously funded. The state had an interest in the ideological upbringing of the young and in presenting the country abroad in the best possible light. Music pedagogy, sport and so on was entirely state-financed. And I was lucky. I had won a few competitions. I was young, my life as a pianist was just beginning. I might have done quite well, I think, but I was living with a foreigner and that jeopardised everything.

If you conformed to the authorities' expectations, and were talented and successful, you were guaranteed a respectable career and a comfortable life. But this was a totalitarian state; if you stepped out of line, or if your circle of friends didn't appeal to the Party and the government, you could end up with no future at all. The pianist Emil Gilels and the violinist David Oistrakh both joined the Communist Party because they felt it was important their talent should not be lost. The same is true of Herbert von Karajan. He was a Nazi, but if he hadn't been he would never have had the chance to build a career. Yes, it's opportunism and it's a pity. But you can't make any kind of judgement from outside. Living there, you see that sometimes there's no way out. To start describing how difficult it is to be yourself in a totalitarian state would be just another platitude.

Of course there are those exceptional cases like Rostropovich: he put his head on the block by defending Solzhenitsyn and the authorities threw him out of the country. They weren't in a position to do more than that to a man of his musical reputation. If you acted freely, you could be forgotten, ignored or expelled.

But by the late 1950s, the Stalinist purges were over, and the 1948 Central Committee Decree, which had denounced Shostakovich, Prokofiev, Khachaturian and others, had been nullified. How seriously were musicians in general affected by political controls and censorship?

In the early years – when the Soviet Union was in its childhood and boyhood the ideologues were far more aggressive and destructive; but, later, when Soviet 'socialism' reached its old age they didn't seem particularly concerned any more.

Censorship was far stricter where the written word and publications were concerned. Not that the employees of the state censorship department *Glavlit* liked to call it that. When *Glavlit* ceased to exist, people who worked there would say 'we weren't censors, we only ever gave an opinion'. In fact, all they needed to do if they saw an unacceptable article was to say to the editor, 'If you publish, you know exactly what'll follow.' There was no need to spell it out. These days they claim that people made their own decisions.

Performers weren't really affected because if you were playing Mozart, it didn't matter as long as you behaved. But just a few members of the Party and the government – those who weren't complete fools – understood that a talent on the scale of, say, Shostakovich offered in musical terms something that could 'corrupt' people's thinking; that it expressed something they didn't want said. You can't put your finger on it. Some Party members understood it, and some didn't care. But those who did see it were afraid not to do anything. And that's where you get the Zhdanov Committee, or Stalin's article about 'Living Music' –

which he was prompted to write by people who were worried about their positions. He went for opera in particular, and Shostakovich and Prokofiev. But this wasn't censorship, it was state policy to root out anything that lay open to interpretation. Because there was so much fear of losing your place in the Central Committee. When Stalin died and things got easier, music lost some of its 'status' and they eased the pressure on composers. But not entirely. Under Khrushchev, there was a composer called Karamanov, for example, who wrote a symphonic cycle with a series of religious titles. He was told that he could keep the symphony but was advised to remove the religious references on the grounds that this would make the work easier to promote and publish. He wasn't banned, he was still performed; but Jesus Christ had to go. The approach became less heavyweight, less zealous, and all the decisions were taken by nervous officials.

You defected in 1963. How did you do it?

I had a concert tour in England and my wife's parents had lived there since 1947 so it was a natural decision to stay. If you're presented with the opportunity to be free, you take it. You couldn't decide to leave while you were in the Soviet Union; you didn't have the right to cross the border.

I had been to the West before so I wasn't as overcome as I had been during my first trip to Brussels in 1956, or when I went on my American tours. But the difference between a short visit, a concert tour even, and living in the West is colossal. It wasn't easy to adapt and become part of a way of life and western society. The complex of relationships between people and the scale of values are poles apart [from those in the USSR]; there's a completely different view of how you should live and behave, and where the priorities should be. I was lucky on two counts. My wife was western – she's Icelandic – and I was 26-years-old. The fact that I was anti-Soviet also helped, of course, but there were plenty of others like that so I was no exception.

The first few months were very difficult. I was lucky in that I had the success I needed so I was spared the material problems. All that was thanks to my musical education, to my teachers – Anaida Sumbatian and Lev Oborin – and quite simply to luck. Success is such a mystery. It's not only luck or training or good performance. There are some imponderable things.

In the West I felt that things moved ahead for me. But I can't say with any certainty that if I'd stayed in Russia I would have made no progress. It's hard to tell – you can't have your life twice over – but I think that if I'd stayed my musical development would have been slower and less wide-ranging. Totalitarianism holds you back: the structure of the society, the opportunities you are offered – everything is hugely constricted.

And how do you feel about the way Russia is going today?

Extremely anxious. Some people say that a nationalist oligarchy could take over, which is not impossible. We can only hope that it won't and that this painful time will lead the country to some kind of democracy. But Russia is so unpredictable politically; at the moment it's all crime, lawlessness and chaos. I see it as a sort of mirror of the Russian character. I'm half Russian and half Jewish myself and I know about the things that go on in me. I know the mentality and the emotions. The political face of a country is a reflection of its peoples' character. In a country as big and influential as this, it's terrifying. Chaos in Russia affects everyone. I'm afraid to travel there. I went just a few months ago. I'll be going to St Petersburg again soon because the orchestra is so good and I'll be conducting. But I go very little these days. I have no sense at all of what the future might hold there. ❏

Interview by **Irena Maryniak**

MZWAKHE MBULI

Freedom puzzle

Is freedom a puzzle?
Is freedom a quiz?
What is freedom?
and what is the meaning of freedom?

To Notsikele Biko the meaning is different
To Helen Suzman the meaning is different
To ex-freedom fighters the meaning is different
What is freedom?
and what is the meaning of freedom

To KwaZulu-Natal people the meaning is different
To Black and White people the meaning is different
To those living in tin shacks the meaning is different
What is freedom?
and what is the meaning of freedom?

To the Bosses and Farmers the meaning is different
To the rich and poor the meaning is different
To the homeless, jobless, miners and workers the meaning is different
What is freedom?
and what is the meaning of freedom?

The SABC and M-Net the meaning is different
To Coca-Cola and Pepsi-Cola the meaning is different
To The Star and Sowetan newspapers the meaning is different.
What is freedom?
and what is the meaning of freedom?

Perhaps freedom is like a jigsaw puzzle
Perhaps freedom is like mirage
Perhaps freedom is wealth for the chosen few

Excerpt from lyrics by Mzwakhe Mbuli. See disc notes p8/9

ROTIMI SANTORRI

From praise to protest

The music of Nigeria's legendary singer and songwriter, Fela Kuti, has its origins in the traditional praise-singing that is an integral part of Yoruba culture and is familiar throughout Africa

The particular genius of Africa's best-known and most colourful musician was to take an ancient and familiar form and transform it into the revolutionary music of Afro-Beat. The history of protest music in Nigeria and much of Africa is the story of the music of Fela Anikulapo Kuti.

Fela was inspired by the Pan-African vision of independent Ghana's first prime minister, Kwame Nkrumah. He wanted to achieve he said, 'the emancipation of all Africans from colonial mentality and second slavery'. And that, he added in 1989, 'is what I am going to die for'. His music became the means to an end. As Fela became politicised through contact with the black civil rights movement in the USA, his music, too, was radicalised. By wedding the racy free-form of the horns, keyboards and strings of jazz to the more syncopated rhythm of African percussion and drums and the hypnotic chanting and repeated call and response of traditional African songs a new, angry sound was created. The result of this fusion was Afro-Beat: a revolutionary sound to carry a revolutionary message.

'We need to use everything we have to fight ignorance, oppression and exploitation. Music is one of the necessary means to carry out the human struggle for a better world. I am an artist, with my music I create change. So really, I am using my music as a weapon. It is conscious,' said Fela in an interview with Carlos Moore in 1989. 'That's why I use politics in my music; that's the only way a wider audience will get acquainted with the important issues.'

Inevitably, this brought Fela into repeated confrontation with the military regimes that ruled Nigeria. His songs were wide-ranging: they advocated the Pan-Africanism of his hero Kwame Nkrumah and 'corrected historical misinformation against black Africans'; defied dictatorships, both military and civilian; opposed persecution and censorship; exposed official corruption; explained the links between political economy and political power. He sang about international politics and neo-colonialism.

His style varied with the issues and his mood. He would question, agitate, advocate, harangue, mock, taunt, satirize, lecture, compare and contrast. Discarding his middle-class background, he used a sharp wit and intellect to break down complex ideas into the pidgin English of the people in the street. Where relevant he would throw in other African languages such as Swahili and Ashanti as well as his native Yoruba.

By the mid 1970's, Nigerias broadcasting authorities had begun to censor Fela's music. Their first move was to label his 'political and confrontational' records 'NTBB' [Not To Be Broadcast] in all radio and TV stations. For most artists this would have been the artistic equivalent of a death sentence. But in anticipation of what the authorities were likely to throw at him, Fela had re-established his night club, The Afro Spot, as The Afrika Shrine. Together with the large compound where he lived, this became known as the Kalakuta Republic, an 'independent republic' within Nigeria and a 'no-go' area for the military.

The Afrika Shrine became Fela's platform where thousands of worshippers thronged to hear the message of dissent from the 'Chief Priest'. For a quarter of a century, except when interrupted by the state or on tour, he played two to five shows a week before activists, students, intellectuals, professionals, workers, artisans, foreign diplomats and fellow musicians. The Shrine was a great leveller and remained the most affordable of 'nite spots'.

In repeated bids to curb his popularity, the Nigerian state apparatus swung into action, charging Fela with everything from possession of illicit drugs (marijuana) to the abduction of young women who had fled from their 'old fashioned' parents to work as singers and dancers in the Shrine. Every attack on Fela produced a counter-attack in song. After unsuccessful attempts to prosecute him in 1973-74, including a spell in the notorious Alagbon police station, his response was the 1974 hit

'Alagbon Close', the lyrics of which have become an anthem against brutality by men in uniform:

> 'For Alagbon/Them no get respect for human beings/Them go send them dog to bite you/Them go point them gun for your face/the gun wey them take your money buy/Them go torture you and take your statement/Them go call am Investigation/Them go lock you for months and months and months and months/Them go call am Investigation...
> Chorus: Nothing special about Uniform/Uniform na cloth na tailor dey sew am...'

By the mid-1970s, recording companies, alarmed by government censorship, were becoming reluctant to release Fela's songs. When Decca Nigeria Limited, which had been acquired by the late politician and media baron Mashood Abiola, reneged on the terms of a contract, Fela responded by occupying Decca's premises with his Afrika 70 Organisation until he had inflicted losses on the company equivalent to the amount owed under the contract. Demands that Fela fulfil other contractual obligations by not making directly anti-government songs, led to the song 'No Agreement':

> 'No Agreement Today/No Agreement Tomorrow/I no go gree/make my brother hungry make I no talk/ ... make my brother homeless make I no talk/my Papa talk/my Mama talk/those wey no talk them dey see/No Agreement Now–Later–Never and Never'

Determined not to allow his 'weapon' to be blunted by the informal censorship of the recording companies, Fela formed his own Kalakuta Records.

In 1977, shortly after the massively attended Festival of Black and African Arts and Culture, FESTAC 77, about 1,000 soldiers armed to the teeth attacked the fortified Kalakuta Republic and razed it to the ground. Millions of naira-worth of equipment was destroyed, men were viciously beaten, singers and dancers were raped. Fela's mother, a hero of the anti-colonial struggle, was thrown from a second-floor window and died shortly after. Fela and the Afrika 70 were gaoled for 'breaching the public peace' and a host of other offences. Kalakuta was seized. A subsequent public inquiry into the incident revealed to a stunned public that the attack was the work of an 'unknown soldier'. Aside from his music, Fela's 'real offence', in the words of one government official, was that he had began to 'take himself too seriously'. He had bought a printing press, established an independent record label, founded a film company that had just completed a controversial film, *The Black President,* and set up a political movement.

On release from prison, Fela's fight back through albums like 'Sorrow Tears and Blood', 'Unknown Soldier' and 'Coffin For Head of State' established him as a legend.

After a brief exile in Ghana, Fela returned in 1978 to re-establish the Shrine and Kalakuta and continued as usual. In 1984, a new military regime jailed him for five years on charges of 'currency trafficking'. A further coup in 1986 released him. He responded to allegations that he had become obssesed with soldiers with:

> 'Some people dey ask foolish question/why I dey put soldier for every song/look every where/[Chr] Soldier dey/for Ministry/Soldier dey/for Sports/Soldier dey/look for Bank/Soldier dey/Even President .../When Armed Robbers come meet you for house/ chop all your food/ fuck all your wives/take all your money/Na so soldier government be...'
> (From the unrecorded 'Music Against Second Slavery').

When Fela died in August 1997, an estimated half a million people attended the wake, the lying in state and burial ceremonies, despite a military ban on large gatherings. Soldiers and police simply stood by. It was a posthumous vote for the man whose many aliases included 'Black President'. ❏

Rohimi Santorri is a Nigerian journalist now living in London

MOKTAR GAOUAD

Committed to rebellion

In an Islamic republic that is sharply divided along class lines and where the conservatives are in control, what artist would not lower her voice? In Mauritania, where certain subjects remain taboo, it's politically unwise to speak up on things that annoy the regime. Even though the last few years have seen a degree of democratic opening and the strengthening of press rights, it has never tolerated free expression,

Malouma Mint El-Meidah is an artist dedicated to opposition. In a society where singers form a cast apart and have, from time immemorial, given their allegiance to the traditional chiefs – on whom the present regime depends to maintain itself in power – she sings of love and excoriates a the nature of her society.

At 38-years-old, she has already been married twice. Her songs take everything on board and her concerts include what are considered 'suggestive' dances. Her hair flows free, a provocation in this 'land of a thousand poets'. In 1988, Mauritania saw serious student riots; Malouma sided with the young people. In 1996, when floods wiped out several of the slums around the capital, Nouakchott, Malouma wrote a song denouncing the outrageous state of the buildings.

The music sung by the *griots* – traditional musicians – of Mauritania is strictly a family afair. Malouma quickly departed from this tradition, forming her own band and introducing modern instruments. While traditional songs follow an unchanging rythm and structure, Malouma 'did something totally different' according to one specialist: 'She reduced compositions that would normally last at least half-an-hour to three or four minutes; that is to say, she sang without regard for the notes and customs of the old music.'

Malouma was born in 1960 into a family of *griots* from around Trarza in south Mauritania. She learned to play the *ardine* – a traditional stringed instrument– at home and sang with her brothers and sisters, several of whom later made careers as soloists.

The role of the *griot* in society is to animate weddings, preserve the history and genealogy of the tribe as well as being its praise-singer. Malouma soon kicked over the traces of this well worn path by parodying Arab classical songs; while Mauritanian songs were in Arabic, the music was played on the instruments of Black Africa. Her songs dwelled on the ills of Mauritanian society. She travelled abroad and exported a modern musical genre in sharp contrast with traditional Mauritanian rythms.

In 1989, following in the wake of other African countries, Mauritania embarked on the road to democracy. Political parties were allowed to form and, in 1992, parliamentary and presidential elections followed. Rival parties centred round the out-going president, Ould Taya, a former colonel in the army who had taken power in a *coup d'état* in 1984, and an opposition coalition led by the former leaders of Mauritania's first regime. Ould Taya was elected with a large majority and his party, the Republican Democratic and Social Party (PRDS) carried off most of the seats in parliament. Ould Taya wiped out an opposition fatally weakened by internal wrangling.

Most sought to consolidate their position with those who had won power and artists who took an opposition position were rare indeed. Among the few who did raise their voices against government, Malouma was far and away the most significant. She became the mouthpiece of the radical opposition. She was there at its meetings and her songs hit the spot more effectively than any of its leaders' speeches.

And so, she was banned. Her songs were forbidden on national radio and television. When UNICEF proposed she should be its ambassador in Mauritania, the authorities countered with a rival proposition, chosing a singer they claimed was 'more moderate'.

'Our society thinks the *griot* has only one role: to serve the tribe,' says Malouma. 'But I see things differently. I have a job to do. I want to do it in a modern way because I want our society to move into the modern world. As a result, the authorities are hostile rather than helpful. I've been 'political' so that I can denounce the collusion between the powers-that-be and this conservative section of our society.'

Malouma says she will never again serve the interests of a tribe or clan. 'The world is changing. Our society too must change. We the *griots* must never again let ourselves be dominated by this old vision of our role. In fact, I wanted my parents to give up this servitude. Put simply: I would like to be at the service of all our people, not promoting the interests of this or that tribe, even my own.'

Malouma is remorseless in her criticism of the government and the conservatives that would hold back the development of society. So far, their only response has been to ignore her and forbid her to express herself freely. However, none of this appears to have tamed or deterred her. She still thinks her 'fight is just and, one day, they will see that I am right'. For the rest, she will leave the future to judge.

Moktar Gaouad is a Mauritanian journalist, working for Radio France Internationale, in Paris. He is one of the original founders of Mauritanie-Nouvelles, *a weekly Mauritanian newspaper which has recently been forced to close by the Nouakchott government*

ISRAEL

Sing it loud
Noam Ven-Zeev

On November 4 1995, Israeli Prime Minister Yitshak Rabin was assassinated by a right-wing youth who opposed the Oslo agreement. Rabin's last words were from Yaacov Rotbliet's 'The Peace Song – a song that was banned when first written and a blood-stained copy of which was found in his pocket. Rotbliet's song became the battle hymn of Israelis seeking peace: 'Don't pray softly for peace, sing it aloud with a great voice'; no more mourning but anger. It expressed their frustration with the country's heroic attitude to war. When a banned song can rise and become almost a second National Anthem, sung at a great gathering for peace by a Prime Minister who, it is said, had never before sung a single note, there is still hope, hope that not even a murderous bullet can extinguish

From diva to driver

For two years, Somalia's national diva, Maryam Mursal, made her living picking up her fans on the streets. For her devoted followers in Mogadishu it was a thrill of a lifetime; for Maryam, having been banned from performing, it was simply a way of surviving: buy a cab, a truck and hustle a living.

Somalia in the 1980s saw general Mohammed Siyed Barre indulge in what the human rights group Africa Watch termed 'terror and indiscriminate slaughter'. Things got too much, even for someone as celebrated as the National Opera's Maryam Mursal. Her song '*Ulimada*', on the surface, innocent enough, was, for those who could read between the lines, a devastating critique of the regime – and the death blow to Maryam's career in Somalia.

She was taken into custody, questioned by police and, following her denial that the song was an overt political comment, released. But, as the song was taken up and openly used by protesters against the regime, she was thrown out of the National Opera and not allowed to perform. Adding insult to injury, the government spread the rumour that Maryam, mother of five and a dedicated Muslim, had performed in a pornographic movie.

It took some years for Maryam to understand what was happening in her civil war-stricken country. Now, more than a decade later, and herself a refugee living in Denmark, she says: 'When I was a big star I couldn't understand why people begged or stole. When the first refugees came to Mogadishu from the north I couldn't accept their begging. Now that I have lost my work and been forced to flee, I have felt persecution and know what it is to be a refugee in my own body: I know what you have to do to survive.' ❏

Ole Reitov

PETER VERNEY

Does Allah like music?

Music possesses a potency within Sudanese society that is sometimes difficult for western cultures to understand

Sudan's National Islamic Front government alternately seeks to oppress music that is unfavourable to the regime through intimidation and force, and then tries to harness its political power by controlling the musicians. Even celebrated 'nationalist' singers from the early days of independence like Mohamed Wardi, Mohamed el-Amin and Abu Araky al-Bakheit have not been spared. Wardi and el-Amin were imprisoned under the dictator Ja'afar Nimeiri in the 1970s; in the early 1990s, the former finally went into exile, certain that he would be a target of the NIF. One of his most celebrated songs commemorates the October 1964 uprising that overthrew General Abboud, independent Sudan's first military dictator.

The songs of Abu Araki al-Bakheit, like those of Wardi, were banned from the airwaves by the NIF and the singer was himself arrested in the early 1990s. On being told by the authorities not to sing his political songs at public gatherings, he opted for total silence. The public outcry eventually prompted him to sing again, in defiance of the authorities, but at the cost of repeated harassment and threats. His only protection is the tremendous respect he is accorded by the Sudanese people. Less famous musicians do not enjoy the same level of protection.

Igd al-Jalad, for instance, a young vocal group formed in the mid-1980s, known for the 'pro-democracy' lyrical content of their songs and the authentic 'roots' quality of their rhythms, have been arrested, threatened and subjected to the ill-treatment that characterises the NIF detention centres known as 'ghost houses'. The group's songs on the

Sudanese musicians – Credit: Adrian Arbib

economic situation and the civil war-induced famine were a particular
cause of concern to the Sudanese authorities. Some members of the
band were detained; others have fled to Cairo.

In general, performers who make any references to past freedoms in
Sudan prior to the 1989 coup are targeted by the government for
harassment and punishment. In one incident, a violinist was taken to the
outskirts of Omdurman and severely beaten by NIF security police.
They smashed his violin and told him to do something religious instead
of playing music. He proceeded to demonstrate, by quotations, that in
fact he knew the Quran better than his tormentors.

The hostility of the NIF towards musicians reflects both the
ambivalent attitude of Islamic teaching towards music and, more
important, the massive popularity of singers whose songs have become

symbolic of the country's desire first for independence (up to 1956) and later for freedom and democracy. The NIF is inherently opposed to the freedom of expression these musicians represent, and views them as dangerous because they could rouse the people against the regime.

The Quran does not itself clearly prohibit music, and music was always important in the cultural life of the Arabs. Some Quranic verses have been interpreted as approving the place of music in human life, while others have been held up as condemning it. The Umayyad Caliphs kept dancers, poets and musicians at their courts. Music and singing matured and developed during this time, with artists such as Ishaq al-Mousli and the composer-singer Ziryab in the early ninth century.

However, under the Abbasid rulers (after 1372), religious disapproval of music and musicians grew. The 'fundamentalist' stance is that music is linked with illicit sex and drinking, and can distract believers from their religious obligations. Dancing is also regarded as an immoral profession.

On the contrary, the Sufi teachers who brought Islam to Sudan made use of musical sounds and dance movements in their forms of religious devotion. Strictly speaking, Quranic recitation, even though it is 'sung', is not regarded by Muslims as music. However, the influence of the Islamic recitation technique on the secular art is unmistakable, and the devotional chanting of the Sufi *Zikr* lies somewhere between the two.

The NIF both fears and seeks to manipulate music and musicians. As a result, periods of repression alternate with periods of coercion, both of them designed to gain control of one of the most potent popular forces in the country. Officials differ in their interpretation and application of the 1990 Public Order Acts which regulate performances: recordings of popular artists may be on sale in the market while the same artists are banned from the airwaves and forbidden to play at wedding parties, the customary venue for music. There have been many incidents of security or public-order police halting wedding parties by arresting the groom or the musicians. The Morality Monitoring Unit of the 'shadow police force', known as the General Administration of Public Order, in addition to clamping down on drug dealers and prostitutes, extends its remit to musical performances at wedding parties. Seven singers were arrested in one week at the beginning of 1993. When a police chief in a northerly town attempted to tighten restrictions on weddings in the same year, however, he provoked three days of mass disturbance.

Intrinsically hostile to the idea of art that it cannot control, the NIF has introduced an 'Islamisation of Art' programme which insists that all performers and works of theatre, cinema and music must be approved by Islamic jurists. The promotion of Islamist ideals and Jihadist songs, notably in praise of the paramilitary Popular Defence Force, is often a principal requirement. Alongside the prohibitions operating on 'low grade' western music there is a general restriction on the diverse range of folk music and dance within the country, which often fails to meet the criteria. The bias that already operated in favour of the Arab-Islamic model to which the northern elites aspired, has gone further than ever in drowning out minority cultural voices, particularly those of the black African south with which it has been at war for the past two decades.

The NIF coup in 1989 was followed by an administrative decree in which the director-general of Radio Omdurman prohibited the broadcast of any song other than those glorifying religion or the National Islamic Front *jihad*. Video and music cassettes of songs mentioning kisses or wine, or with political allusions, have been erased and pro-NIF speeches and religious sermons recorded over them. Large amounts of irreplaceable studio archive material has been lost in this way. In 1992, for example, the controllers of Radio Juba wiped its tapes of the celebrated southern Sudanese singer Yousif Fataki, and used them for public addresses by President Omar Bashir.

Extensive radio and television air-time has been given to rebroadcasting fierce verbal assaults on artists by speakers at NIF mosques. The makers of non-religious music have been denounced as morally corrupting, and an atmosphere of hysteria and intolerance has been fostered, culminating in the murder of popular singer Khogali Osman in November 1994 when a man gained admission to the Musicians' and Singers' Club in Omdurman and stabbed Khojali to death and injured several others, including the internationally known Abdel Qadir Salim.

The Musicians' Union in Khartoum appealed for airtime to redress the imbalance and defend their music, but was threatened with reprisals against musicians and their families by security officers. ❑

Peter Verney is the editor of Sudan Update, *an independent information service supported by international humanitarian and human rights organisations*

DANIEL BROWN

Dance, dance wherever you may be

Early in 1997, Tabu Ley Rochereau, one of Africa's most celebrated musicians and an integral part of the Golden Age of Congo-Zairean music in the 1960s, released 'Kebo Beat', a penetrating yet humorous look at the realities his country faced in the final days of the reign of Mobutu Sese Seko, one of Africa's most vicious and imperious dictators in recent history. It was yet another landmark in Rochereau's 43-year musical career.

As has often been the case in the 1,500 compositions he's accredited with, Rochereau focuses on the social and sensual habits of his fellow Congolese. As well as denouncing the arrogance of the rich in his defence of the poor ('*Eh M'vuama*') and finding hope in the gathering momentum of a rebellion in the east led by Laurent-Desiré Kabila in '*Kibomama*', in '*Je m'en fous*' he satirises male-female relationships and in '*Mil Mi Nef Sa*' (1,900AD), recounts in Lingala the innate desire to dance:

> 'The day rises hiding our daily problems,/My profession is musician, a gift from God,/My job is to sing and make people dance/Since the beginning of time everyone dances/Let the one who can't dance raise his hand/Some do it in the bar, some in the nightclubs/And there are ones who dance and grind in the bedroom'.

It was the last line that particularly inflamed the new authorities and landed Tabu Ley in trouble.

Within months of Kabila's military victory and his arrival in the capital, Kinshasa, Rochereau ended his 10-year exile in the USA and returned home. Politically sympathetic to Kabila, he quickly relayed his desire to become involved in the cultural politics of his nation as it approached, he believed, the dawn of a new era. 'I'm at a crossroads of my life,' he explains in a telephone interview from Kinshasa. 'I came back here after a decade in exile to work for my people and unite all the artists in a new vision of the arts. But the minister of culture wants to destroy me.'

'Kebo Beat' was banned from the airwaves and record stores in Congo for what the authorities called 'morally incorrect language and imagery'. The official press has attacked the veteran singer as an 'obscene musician', focusing on '*Mil Mi Nef Sa*' as 'moral-sapping'. 'It's disgusting,' rages Rochereau. 'I'm being treated like some sort of criminal. After all these years of fighting Mobutu, they are calling me an unhealthy influence, contaminated by the West.'

It is not clear who Rochereau means by 'they', since the 58-year-old claims to have the ear of Kinshasa's new strongman, Kabila. But it seems the composer is not the only musician targeted by the ministry. Congolese superstar Koffi Olomide, came under fire for 'SOS', a track on his latest album, 'Loi'. Initially threatened with a ban on the distribution of the album unless he removed the offending track, Olomide finally succeed in getting 'SOS' reinstated, but not before he had taken the fight all the way up to the Congolese Censorship Commission.

'SOS' appears even more anodyne than Tabu Ley's offending lyric but, according to Congolese journalist Kasongo Mwema, 'Ever since certain *zouk* artists began to sing explicit lyrics on men/women behaviour, the authorities have decided to crack down on the slightest sexual innuendo. They've gone from one extreme to another.' The song describes a woman, betrayed by her man, leaving her with their child.

'You promised me the moon, I'm still in love, in love/I'd do anything to keep you/Don't forget the good things we shared together/You'll be responsible for my death/I can't survive this/This unrequited lust nourished from such high hopes/I'll never survive such grief.' ❏

Daniel Brown *is a journalist at Radio France International (RFI).*

KRISTER MALM

A world of lost music

Throughout Africa, musicians have been trapped in bondage by a combination of national cultural policies, poverty and exploitative businessmen. In the case of Patrick Balisidaya of Tanzania, it was the government who played exploiter

In 1976–78 one of the most popular bands in Tanzania was Afro 70 Band led by composer/musician Patrick Balisidya. In 1977, as Tanzania's representatives at FESTAC 77 in Nigeria, Afro 70 was given new instruments by the Tanzanian government. In 1978, the band lost their government-owned instruments in a car accident during a tour in Tanzania. Balisidya was held responsible for the loss of the instruments, even accused of stealing them. There was no trial nor conviction then or in later years; for 20 years one of Africa's finest musicians has been the victim of a vengeful and uncaring government bureaucracy.

In 1979, Balisidya came to Sweden and recorded an album with the Swedish group *Arkimedes Badkar* (Archimedes' Bathtub) on the MNW label. It was one of the first albums of what later became known as 'world music' and the hope was that its sales would provide the money to replace the lost instruments. But world music was not yet the fashion and Balisidya had to return to Tanzania without the new instruments when his visa expired.

Even though fellow musicians rate him one of the most gifted musicians in African popular music, Balisidya has been on an unofficial blacklist in Tanzania for 20 years, deprived of making his living as a musician. He has proved his gifts on many audio cassettes made in the 1980s and 1990s but, given the blacklist, no major record company has dared back him. His songs are big hits in East Africa and have been recorded by other bands, but nobody has yet defied the ban and hired Balisidya in Tanzania. Nor has he been able to get the necessary backing to emigrate.

In November 1997, Balisidya was pinning his hopes on the new Tanzanian government; it would help him get new instruments and set up a band again. But he has lost 20 creative years. His spirit is broken and world music has lost what might have been one of its leading music makers. ❑

Krister Malm is a musicoligist and Director of the National Museum of Music in Stockholm

OLE REITOV

White Zulu

The term 'white Zulu' is synonymous with Johnny Clegg, South Africa's first world music chart buster. White Zulu because Clegg, anthropologist as well as musician, mastered the Zulu language culture, dance and music at an early age and, in the 1980s, became a symbol for white South Africans who fought alongside black friends for a new, democratic, multicultural South Africa. It was Clegg' s superb blend of Zulu music and western pop that made him and his groups *Juluka* and *Savuka* household names in the West.

His music was often banned and his shows tear-gassed by South African security forces. Solidarity movements in the West didn't know what to do; Clegg was breaking the cultural boycott against South Africa long before Paul Simon was even thinking of recording with South African musicians.

Throughout this time Clegg remained outspoken in the conviction that for all its obvious downside, censorship was responsible for sparking off the creativity that distinguished his work. 'It pushed you to find ways around it and suddenly you realised that you were inventing a whole new grammar for yourself. Then your followers began to decipher this and so you always had this special communication in live shows because people had started to understand.

Clegg used his albums to comment on South African society, but his first group, *Juluka*, fought on the cultural rather than political front. 'We had spectacular dancing and celebrated different cultures with a group of people who came from different tribes, different races and so on. That was the key thing.' His second group, *Savuka*, was more overtly political: the lyrics of their 'Third World Child' constituted a political manifesto and, inevitably, was banned – 'restricted' – by the South African Broadcasting Corporation (SABC). And made the charts in France, the UK and the US.

Clegg's own first encounter with the West in 1972 was a profound cultural shock. 'We grew up in the hippie era and we saw these guys saying and doing the most outrageous things openly. You were 16 and you saw a guy on TV smoking dope or saying 'fuck the Queen'. It was a very shocking experience because this was completely impossible in our society.'

While South African theatre became a potent, radical force, according to Clegg, music turned the other cheek. 'We had great political theatre, a whole genre of rage, music went the other way. Music was about healing, finding ways in which a sound would give you five minutes in a safe place, a cocoon of harmony. Young music is about rebellion, about youthful anger pushing at the limits, breaking down boundaries, attacking the status quo, overturning conventional wisdom, finding its own way. That was never allowed here. So we imposed very tame mixes and lyrical expression on ourselves. It's the emotional and ideological result of self-censorship on writing or performing in this country,

Life in the new South Africa raises a lot questions on freedom of expression and Clegg is in no way a promoter of total 'free expression'. 'Censorship raises many interesting questions. I am strongly against child pornography, for instance; against racist and hate speech. These are areas that have to be closely examined and clearly articulated; all extremes are bad, especially when you are at a fragile stage in the development of a global information culture. We are all at an infantile stage at the moment and we have to find a way to bring a maturity to the way information is produced, disseminated, controlled, and experienced,' he says, concluding, 'I think freedom of expression and freedom of access are quite hollow without equal access.' ❑

CECILE PRACHER

Only doing my duty

'I was just doing a job and I didn't see anything wrong in that. I thought it was the right thing to do,' says Cecile Pracher, manager of the South African Broadcasting Corporation's (SABC) record library.

indly note that the undermentioned vocal items MAY NOT BE USED IN ANY
ROGRAMME OF THE SABC's SERVICES:

. "ASIMBONANGA"   (J CLEGG)
  BY: JOHNNY CLEGG AND SAVUKA   MINC MINC(0) 4051461
  LP: JOHNNY CLEGG & SAVUKA

. "I WASN'T THERE (But I can feel the Pain)" (R HAMMOND)
  BY: ROY C   MERCURY VRL 1016
  LP: SOUL

. "I'M GONNA LOVE SOMEBODY ELSE'S WOMAN"   (R HAMMOND)
  (Somebody's lovin' mine)   (MERCURY VRL 1016)
  BY: ROY C
  LP: SOUL

. "OPEN LETTER TO THE PRESIDENT"   (R HAMMOND)
  BY: ROY C   MERCURY VRL 1016
  LP: SOUL

. "THE WORLD IN WHICH WE LIVE"   (WANG CHUNG)
  BY: WANG CHUNG   GEFFEN GFC 1005
  LP: MOSAIC

he undermentioned LP MAY NOT BE USED IN ANY PROGRAMME OF THE SABC's
ERVICES:

. LP: INFECTED   (M JOHNSON)
  BY: THE THE   EPIC KSF 3138

ROELF JACOBS
GENERAL MANAGER: ENGLISH AND AFRIKAANS RADIO GROUP

Room 601
Ext 2700

For years she attended the weekly meetings of the SABC Censor Board Committee, first as a junior in the 'white section', later as library manager. Station managers were seldom involved in discussions; records the committee decided to ban, or in the words of the official notification 'restrict', were simply spoiled beyond use by scratching with a nail and a list of 'restricted records' was circulated to managers and presenters.

'Many other sections in the SABC, especially the news departments, were highly politicised and often had visits from intelligence, but we did our work so efficiently no-one had to interfere,' says Cecile, 'neither intelligence nor the publications board – it was involved with wholesale banning, literature, music, pamphlets, t-shirts, you name it – bothered us.'

Today, she's not particularly proud of the scratchings or of the censorship itself. 'Once you're outside a situation it's difficult to understand how you could have been led by the nose for so long. But then we were so polarised and now we have difficulties in getting to grips with what we went through. 'That's why we're asking: why is it that some people did see the light? As far back as 1964 there was an Afrikaaner preacher, the head of the Broederbond, who nevertheless had the courage to move away from the whole Afrikaaner dogma. And they crucified him for it. But most of us were more a group following the herd.'

Some of the censors were doing rather more than 'just their job' says Cecile, but most were 'quite objective' given their own limitations, the nature of the job and their role. Sometimes it would 'hurt' to ban a song, especially when these were by Afrikaans singer-songwriters like David Kramer and Anton Goosen. 'This was painful.'

But all the time they were banning, censors were enjoying at home songs they had banned at work. 'It was playing one role in one place and another somewhere else and not feeling schizophrenic about it,' says Cecile. 'It angers me. The whole conflict of morality and the way it was enforced angers me.'

And she continues: 'People won't take on the responsibility of turning around and saying we screwed up but that we did what we did because we thought we were right for whatever reason. Even now the politicians in this country won't take it on: it's always somebody else. I'd be the first to say that of course I was part of the elitist whites in this country. But it was a frame of mind; it was comfortable. But the brainwashing. I can't believe it's possible to brainwash five million people and, on top of everything, use the church and religion to get across a message calling for the total destruction of another part of the country, of people that should be close to you.'

In Cecile Pracher's opinion it would be a good thing if South Africa had a Truth Commission on music and culture to match the commission now examining the political and personal abuses committed under apartheid. The damage to music was enormous, and she doesn't want censorship back in any form. 'Except where children are concerned any form of censorship is bad. For adults censorship is bad news.'

'It's amazing how easily humans can adapt to a new system,' says the former censor, who now listens to a far wider range of music and remembers the past with bitterness. 'In addition to the whole business of censorship we were very much forced into our cubicles and kept there. If you listened to the Afrikaans or English service you wouldn't have dreamed of listening to black music. Johnny Clegg was the first to cross over. That cross-pollination was the greatest loss in every aspect of our life. We were totally separated, each of us on our own little island. ❏

Cecile Pracher *was interviewed by Ole Reitov*

No fear for the wicked

Governments have far more to fear than individuals when it comes to drawing a line under the past. Relatives have often confronted the worst as they worried, mourned or hoped in vain for some word of their loved ones or confirmation of their last resting places. Long before the matter arrives before whatever court has been convened to 'disappear' such lapses from the nation's psyche, their personal grief – like the body of evidence itself – has been shallow-buried, awaiting only for the legal specialist to disinter it, apportion guilt and, ultimately, to apologise.

The circumstances under which a dissident meets his or her death at the hands of a régime of state terror, are entirely at odds with those that lead its successor to disentangle past evils and bring the perpetrators into the light of day. Whether the grieving family has 'moved on' or not, the government almost invariably has, either into the moral uplands that accompanied the setting up of a Truth and Reconciliation Commission as in South Africa, or to face the challenges of democratic governance that followed hard on the heels of the nightmare in Chile. These changed realities provide a wealth of pretexts for dodging the hardest political choice of all: whether to press charges against the guilty, even though time and political compromise have lent them a patina of respectability, sometimes even statesmanship.

Whether the case at issue is the extradition of Augusto Pinochet of Chile or the continuing process of reconciliation in South Africa, October was a sorry month for those who believe it is possible to establish a uniform code of practise for dealing with gross violations of human rights. The need to weigh the competing demands for criminal prosecution against reconciliation through some form of truth commission has been well documented (*Index* 3/1998). The ANC decided on a two-and-a-half year public confession by those on both sides of the *apartheid* barrier, but then balked at releasing a final document that had equally harsh words for high-ranking members of its own cabinet.

But the route to criminal prosecution is also fraught. On 17 July in Rome, Britain had been among 120 countries to sign an undertaking to establish an international criminal court, endorsing the principle that there can be no impunity, amnesty or sovereign immunity for 'crimes committed against humanity'. Less than four months later, a London High Court used a fig-leaf in the, perhaps, aptly-named Criminal Justice Bill of 1988 to reject Spanish demands for the extradition of Pinochet on the grounds that, as a former head of state, the former dictator enjoyed 'sovereign immunity' on British soil.

For all the furore it aroused, the Pinochet case was complicated by the fact that the call for legal redress came not from Chileans for whom the price of democracy in a 1988 plebiscite had been renunciation of any final resolution as to who was responsible for the death of some 3,000 people in custody. It came instead from Spain, which is seeking justice for the scores of Spanish citizens murdered during the Chilean dictatorship. Though it is unlikely that the magistrate concerned could produce *prima facie* evidence implicating the general himself, the object of the indictment was to make him accountable for crimes that occurred during his time in office.

In ruling that Pinochet was not liable in the UK, the British court was reiterating its refusal to extend its jurisdiction into the internal affairs of a foreign state – and underlining the inherently fictive nature of the government's 'ethical' foreign policy. The decision, perhaps, was influenced by the reluctance to permit the judiciary to become the channel for possibly interminable claims against distant, formerly friendly dictators.

But could an international criminal court better serve the individual than the Truth and Reconciliation Commission in South Africa, or the courts of Spain or Britain? The size of the vote in favour was probably the strongest indication that that it will not. For, when push comes to shove, few governments will give real assent to a body with powers to litigate retroactively and across borders. ❏

Michael Griffin

A censorship chronicle incorporating information from the American Association for the Advancement of Science Human Rights Action Network (AAASHRAN), Amnesty International (AI), Article 19 (A19), the BBC Monitoring Service Summary of World Broadcasts (SWB), the Committee to Protect Journalists (CPJ), the Canadian Committee to Protect Journalists (CCPJ), the Inter-American Press Association (IAPA), the International Federation of Journalists (IFJ/FIP), the International Federation of Newspaper Publishers (FIEJ), Human Rights Watch (HRW), the Media Institute of Southern Africa (MISA), International PEN (PEN), Open Media Research Institute (OMRI), Reporters Sans Frontières (RSF), the World Association of Community Broadcasters (AMARC), the World Organisation Against Torture (OMCT) and other sources

ALBANIA

On 8 September **Agron Bala**, director of Tirana-based Radio Kontakt and host of a popular chat show, was attacked by unknown assailants when leaving the studio. (RSF)

ALGERIA

On 11 October *La Nation* reappeared on news stands after nearly two years of suspension for 'non-payment of printers fees' (*Index* 1/1996, 3/1996). Former editor **Salima Ghezali**, who has won both the Olof Palme and Sakharov prizes, resumed her post, though she now presides over a weekly rather than a daily and a greatly reduced staff. A second banned independent weekly, *El-*

Houria (Liberty), also resumed publication recently. (*Le Monde*)

ARGENTINA

On 16 August the Supreme Court refused **Carmen Aguiar de Lapaco**'s petition for access to the military and civilian archives in an attempt to trace her daughter, who disappeared in the 'dirty war'. (Equipo Nizkor)

Journalist **Olga Wornat** was sacked from her programme at Radio FM Horizonte on 19 August, two weeks after a judge assigned her two bodyguards after a series of threatening phone calls. Wornat is writing a book critical of Carlos Menem's presidency. (Freedom Forum)

On 20 August Radio Belgrano journalist Eduardo Aliverti was sentenced to pay US$50,000 to ex-civil servant Juan Jose Ramos for reading on air an article from the magazine *El Porteno* which accused Ramos of requesting a commission to regulate radio advertising. Ramos was unsuccessful in his previous lawsuit attempt against Jorge Latana, director of *El Portero* magazine. (Periodistas)

On 24 August court-room images from the 1985 trial of members of the military junta during the 'dirty war' were for the first time shown on TV. An estimated 3 million viewers tuned into *ESMA: the Day of the Trial* (the building housing ESMA, the intelligence service, served as a detention and torture centre). (Freedom Forum)

AUSTRALIA

A judge asked the government to set up an inquiry into the deaths of five journalists in East Timor 23 years ago, after publication of a report by the International Commission of Jurists (ICJ) on 24 August. The Geneva-based ICJ said Indonesian troops killed Australian newsmen **Greg Shackleton** and **Tony Stewart**, Britons **Malcolm Rennie** and **Brian Peters** and New Zealander **Gary Cunningham** in the western village of Balibo in October 1975 to keep their invasion of the island under wraps. The *Sydney Morning Herald* said on 24 August that it had found evidence that Australian diplomats had been briefed on the plan to attack Balibo three days before it occurred. (Reuters)

AZERBAIJAN

On 15 August 7 *Gyun* correspondent **Sahkil Kerimli**, *525 Gazeta* employees **Mustafa Gajily** and **Aydyn Bagirov**, and **Natig Javadly** and **Fizuli Dovlyatov** of *Olailar* were arrested and had their films destroyed by police while covering an opposition rally in Baku. **Babek Bekir**, a correspondent for the Azeri service of Radio Liberty, and **Eldanis Elgyun** of ANS-TV were detained on the same day in Gyanja. (RSF, Glasnost Defence Foundation, RFE/RL)

Two people, including a police officer, have been arrested for an assault on opposition journalist **Haji Zamin** on 22 August. Zamin, a correspondent for the Azerbaijan Popular Front newspaper *Azadliq*, was beaten and subjected to verbal abuse at a metro station in Baku. (Human Rights Centre of Azerbaijan, RFE/RL)

Police prevented reporters from ANS and Space TV from covering a 26 August picket by 140 municipal workers in Sumqayit who were protesting about working conditions and non-payment of their salaries. (Human Rights Centre of Azerbaijan)

On 1 September **Tale Hamid**, editor of the independent newspaper *Mustagil*, was dragged from his car and beaten by four policemen for attempting to drive down a road that President Heidar Aliyev's motorcade was scheduled to use 90 minutes later. (RSF)

Thirty-four journalists were beaten by police as they covered a banned rally in Baku on 12 September, that called for the cancellation of the 11 October presidential elections. Many had recording and camera equipment taken or broken. It was also reported that police tried to break into a building housing independent and opposition media, including the newspapers *Azadliq* and *Chag*, and the Turan news agency. (Human Rights Centre of Azerbaijan, CPJ, RSF)

Two sisters on the staff of the opposition newspaper *Yeni Musavat*, **Esmira** and **Ilhama Namiqqizi**, were attacked at Ahmedly metro station in Baku on the evening of 30 September. A day earlier, Esmira Namiqqizi had

published an article criticising officers in the Interior Ministry's Anti-Gangster and Anti-Terrorism Department. Rauf Arifoglu, editor of *Yeni Musavat*, said the paper had received 'numerous' threatening telephone calls (*Index* 4/1998). (RFE/RL)

The publisher of a new English-language paper, *Baku Sun*, pulled the first issue on 5 October lest its contents annoy the government. US publisher **James Phillipoff** said he made the decision after officials at the Azerbaijani Communications Ministry complained about two articles: 'Aliyev vows to keep order' and 'Humans retreat as Azerbaijan's rat population flourishes'. (Reuters)

It was reported on 11 August that UNESCO is investigating the blacklisting of **Hussa Al Khumairi** by the Ministry of Education following her refusal to retract her name from a women's pro-democracy petition in 1995 which called for the restoration of the National Assembly and an end to abuses by the security forces. UNESCO granted Al Khumairi an honorary medal for her work in adult education. (Bahrain Freedom Movement)

On 26 August **Huda Al Safaf** was summoned to an interrogation centre and accused of selling books from her home. (Bahrain Freedom Movement)

At least one person, a teenager called **Yasser**, was arrested for speaking to the BBC journalists who accompanied UK Foreign

Minister Derek Fatchett on his visit on 14 September, it was reported 12 days later. (Bahrain Freedom Movement)

On 5 August **Dipak Chowdhury**, a reporter for *Dainik Muktakantha*, was assaulted by a Dhaka constable just after entering the Bangladesh Secretariat that houses various ministries. Other journalists intervened to protect him. (RSF)

After writing about the armed Chattra League (CL) cadres at Dhaka University, **Kailash Sarkar**, correspondent for the daily *Sanba*, and **Mamun**, correspondent for the daily *Janakantha*, received death threats from Ebadat Hossain, a CL leader on 10 August. (Media Watch)

On 23 August **Rehnuma Ahmed**, Assistant Professor of Anthropology at Jahangir Nagar University, and a respected member of the Drik Picture Library, was assaulted by cadres of the government's student organisation while she was taking pictures of their rally to protest against the lack of investigation into the rape of three women students. (*Daily Star*)

Saiful Alam Mukul, editor of the *Daily Runner*, was killed by gunmen on 30 August in the eastern Jessore district. The *Daily Runner* had published stories critical of the outlawed East Bangla Comunist Party in the Jessore area. (Media Watch, RSF, CPJ)

On 17 September it was reported that the writer **Taslima Nasrin** (*Index* 10/1993, 3/1994, 4/1994, 5/1994, 6/1994, 1/1995, 2/1995, 6/1996, 2/1997) had returned from four years of exile, and promptly gone into hiding after Islamic groups recommenced protests against her for blasphemy. On 5 October Foreign Minister Abdus Samad Azad made the government's first public statement on the case when he said that 'the religious sentiment of the people should be respected, but we cannot allow any excesses in the name of religion.' Nasrin still faces criminal charges. (*The Times,* RSF, CCPJ, International Pen)

BELARUS

On 21 August a Minsk district court sentenced Bishop **Pyotr Hushcha**, leader of the Orthodox Autocephalous Church, to three years for 'malicious hooliganism'. Huscha was arrested for allegedly exposing himself to two young girls. The bishop claimed the case was fabricated to discourage others from challenging the 'domination of the Russian Orthodox Church'. (RFE/RL)

BOSNIA-HERZEGOVINA

On 29 July a bomb exploded close to the Sarajevo office of the biweekly magazine *Dani,* causing considerable damage. *Dani* recently published articles linking the mafia and the authorities, most notably the ruling Party of Democratic Action. (RSF)

On 12 August Republika Srpska Information Minister Rajko Vasic said the government had ordered the closure of the Pale-based Bosnian Serb news agency SRNA. He said the decision was made because of SRNA's 'fabrications, tendentious reporting, and manipulating of the speeches of top officials'. (RFE/RL)

On 7 September Robert Berry, chairman of the temporary Electoral Commission, banned Deputy Serbian Prime Minister Vojislav Seselj from any further involvement in the September Republika Srpska elections. The ultra nationalist was prevented from speaking publicly and participating in political rallies after he used offensive terms to describe ethnic Albanians and indulged in 'slanderous accusations' against the leaders of other political parties. (RFE/RL)

BRAZIL

Investigative TV journalist **Donizete Adauto** was shot dead on 18 September by a group of gunmen. Adauto had received death threats that related to his investigations of the dealings of politicians and businessmen. He was also a candidate for the federal congress in the presidential elections of 4 October. (Associated Press, Freedom Forum)

BULGARIA

On 6 September authorities permitted circumcision ceremonies for 30 Muslim boys in the Teke mosque, Dobrich.

The practice had hitherto been banned. (RFE/RL)

BURMA

On 7 August British student **James Mawdsley** was released and deported after serving three months in a central Rangoon jail. He was sentenced to five years' imprisonment after being caught with pro-democracy leaflets. (*Independent*)

On 12 August Italian journalist **Maurizio Giuliano** was stopped by custom officials who confiscated his films, tapes and some notes. (IFJ)

French journalist **Romian Franklin** was arrested on 17 August as he was leaving the opposition NLD headquarters. Accused of having entered the country illegally, he was put on the first flight to Bangkok, after his film and tapes were confiscated. (RSF)

On 18 August the authorities denounced the BBC, Voice of America and Radio Free Asia for interfering in internal affairs by 'profusely advocating the demands of the lady [Aung San Suu Kyi]'. (Reuters, RSF)

CAMBODIA

The government announced on 15 October that it intended to shut down two English language newspapers and expel their US and British journalists. (*Far East Economic Review*)

CAMEROON

On 31 July it was reported that the family of imposoned editor and journalist **Pius Njawe**

(*Index* 3/1998, 4/1998, 5/1998) have received anonymous death threats. Western diplomats also testified in an unofficial memorandum that the 'physical elimination' of the journalist had been contemplated. (RSF)

Michel Michaut Moussala, editor of the privately owned *Aurore Plus* publication, was arrested on 3 September and is being held in the New Bell Prison. Moussala's arrest follows a six-month jail sentence in January for publishing an article questioning President Paul Biya's health (*Index* 2/1998). (RSF)

CANADA

Police have begun to investigate Prime Minister Jean Chrétien's role in silencing protesters at last year's Asia Pacific economic summit in Vancouver, after documents leaked by the Royal Canadian Mounted Police in September revealed that officials accompanying ex-president Suharto wanted to know what would happen if they shot protesters. (*Index* 2/1998). The prime minister's office responded on 16 October by accusing CBC reporter **Terry Milewski** of bias in his reporting of the story. (*Globe and Mail*)

Industry minister John Manley unveiled on 1 October new cryptography guidelines that encourage Canadians to develop and import powerful data-scrambling technologies, contrary to US policy The authorities do not require users to submit to mandatory key recovery, which would make all scrambled communications accessible to the government. (*Wired News*)

Recent publications: *Trivia Pursuit: How Showbiz Values are Corrupting the News*, by Knowlton Nash (McClelland & Stewart); *Yesterday's News: Why Canada's Daily Newspapers are Failing Us*, by John Miller (Fernwood).

CHAD

On 20 July **Yorongar Ngarléjy le Moiban**, a member of the National Assembly and the political opposition party the FAR, was sentenced to three years for defaming President Déby and the President of the National Assembly, Wadal Abdelkader Kamougué. Two journalists from *L'Observateur*, **Sy Koumbo Singa Gali** and **Polycarpe Togamissi**, were convicted of complicity in the defamation and recieved two-year suspended sentences and CFAFr1 million (around US$1,600) fines. The judge who tried the case was previously a member of the prosecution team that had brought the charges. *L'Observateur* published an interview in which Ngarléjy accused Kamougué of accepting money from French oil company Elf to finance his presidential electoral campaign. (AI)

CHILE

Daily newspaper *La Epoca*, established in 1987 and once considered the 'champion of democracy', ceased publication on 30 July. The paper began to lose its importance in 1990, when it became the informal mouthpiece of the Christian Democrat party. (Freedom Forum)

Student **Claudia Alejandra López Benange** was shot to death by police on 11 September during a public demonstration with 40 other people. On the day of her funeral, journalists were detained and others were prevented from taking photographs. (Derechos)

CHINA

Outspoken radio journalist **Albert Cheng** was attacked by men wielding carving knives as he walked into the studios of Kowloon's Commercial Radio station on 19 August. Police said the attacks may have been carried out by people who felt offended by the 'cutting' remarks about politics and the economy that he vents on his top-rated programme *Teacup in a Storm*. (*New York Times*)

Policemen arrested CBS TV producer **Natalie Liu** at her home on 2 September and seized her videotapes and photographs. Liu, who is married to a US citizen, was not told why she had been arrested, but sources say it is because she had been working for CBS without official approval. (RSF)

Delight over the publication of a path-breaking book on political reform in China subsided after one of its editors was arrested. *Political China: Facing the era of choosing a new structure* brings together 39 essays on corruption and the

●●●●●●●●●●●●●●●●●●●●●●●●●●●●●●●

CARLOS REYES

The General and I

What torturers try to do is strip you of all dignity. They would play me tapes of babies screaming, and tell me that I was hearing the sound of my own children. They would say that they would be killed if I did not cooperate. They wanted the names of people in the party, but I had none to give. They forced me to do heavy manual labour for days on end. You are so tired you cannot sleep at night. Then they don't feed you for days, you are deprived of water and basic human needs. They would just treat me like I was any animal. My torturers saw me as someone who had given up the right to be human.

You start to think that your life has lost all meaning, as if there's nothing worth living for. I was beaten up all the time. It often took the form of severe torture. They would punch and kick me around in groups. I was hit with sticks and anything they could find that would cause pain.

When I heard that Pinochet has been arrested, I feel like I wanted to cry. I don't see his arrest as a personal victory, it is justice for the thousands who went missing. They have to be found. They were all friends of mine, some were fellow journalists. Some of them have been killed and their families wiped out. I was lucky, I escaped. But I will always remember what it feels like to be tortured and at the mercy of people who know not to care.

It will take this country years to get over Pinochet's legacy. Finding out what happened to his victims is where we should begin. ❏

Carlos Reyes was a freelance journalist and member of Chile's Socialist Party in 1974, when he was arrested by General Augusto Pinochet's security apparatus and tortured for two years. He escaped in 1979 and is now president of the human rights group Chile Democratico. On 28 October, the High Court in London ruled the 82-year-old former president was immune from arrest and extradition to Spain on charges of genocide and torture because he was 'entitled to immunity as a former sovereign, from criminal and civil process in the English courts'. From the Guardian, *October 1998*

●●●●●●●●●●●●●●●●●●●●●●●●●●●●●

political system by dissident journalists, scholars and former government officials. Co-editor **Shi Binhai** was arrested in Beijing by security agents on 5 September 1998. Agents searched his home and seized audio tapes, photographs and notebooks, while his family were warned not to tell anybody about his detention. Shi was previously arrested in 1989 for his role in the Tiananmen Square demonstrations and had worked as senior editor for the *China Economic Times*. (RSF)

COLOMBIA

On 11 August **Luiz Amparo Jimenez Pallares** was shot in the head three times by a man who escaped in a vehicle driven by an accomplice. He was correspondant for the TV news programme *En Vivo* and also worked for the non-governmental organisation Redepaz (Network for initiatives for peace and against war). Jimenez Pallares had received death threats since taking part in a documentary about peasants displaced from land in 1996 which was later appropriated by a government official. (CPJ, RSF)

On 27 August journalist **Nelson Osorio Patiño** was shot twice in the head by a man who fled from the killing on a motorcycle. Osorio was producer of the *Gran Prix* sports programme in Senal, owner of a regional sports paper and a sports reporter. (CPJ, RSF)

CUBA

On 23 July *Cuba Prensa Libre*

issued its first English-language version under the title of *Cuba Free Press*. (*Cuba Free Press*)

On 28 July **Raúl Rivero Castañeda**, director of the independent news agency *Cuba Press*, was picked up by security officials and interrogated. Rivero Castañeda, a respected poet, was again detained on 12 August, only to be released without charge three days later. (Cuba Net)

On 28 August dissident **Reinaldo Alfaro García**, a member of the Democratic Solidarity Party, was sentenced to three years in prison for disseminating 'false information', the first conviction of its kind since Pope John Paul's visit in January. Last year Alfaro García sent a letter to parliament demanding freedom for political prisoners. He later spoke on the US's Radio Martí about their health. (*Contacto*)

Cuba Press journalist **Juan Antonio Sánchez Rodriguez** was detained on 10 September in Havana and taken to State Security headquarters. He remains in prison without being charged. (RFS)

Manuel Antonio González, another *Cuba Press* journalist, was detained on 1 October and accused of 'offending' President Castro. Members of his family have also been targeted in recent violent attacks. (RSF)

DEMOCRATIC REPUBLIC OF CONGO

Three accredited members of a World Television Network

crew, **Michael Pohl**, **Michael Higgins** and **Jonathan Kolionio**, were detained on 23 August and held incommunicado for two days on the orders of the minister of information. Other visiting journalists have been similarly harassed, according to a 26 August report.

Hugh Nevill, special correspondent for Agence France Presse, and *Newsweek*'s **Lara Santoro** were questioned at the Zambian border as they were speaking by satellite telephone with the secretary of the province of Katanga. Similarly, **Roger Roy** and **Sipo Maseko**, cameramen with Reuters Television, were detained for several hours for filming in the streets of Kinshasa. (IFJ)

On 5 September, a group of armed guards forcibly entered the offices of the privately owned *La Rue Meurt* and removed the weekly's computer equipment. The authorities offered no explanation. (RSF)

It was reported on 21 September that security officials had arrested seven journalists with state radio in Kinshasa, on charges that they had formed a support committee for rebels. The same journalists had been arrested the previous week but were released after the intervention of the information minister. (Agence France Presse, IRIN)

EGYPT

On 2 August an administrative court ruled that the Information Ministry ban on the publication of newspapers in the free zones was illegal and unconstitutional, noting that it damaged even 'responsible' publications (*Index* 3/1998, 4/1998). (*Cairo Times*)

On 12 and 19 August, the authorities confiscated and banned distribution of the first two issues of the Cyprus-based cultural weekly *Alf Layla* for drawing parallels between a recent film on former president Gamal Abdel Nasser and a pornographic film made in 1980s by the same director, **Anwar al Qawadri**. The paper was informed that it had portrayed 'the leaders of Egypt in the context of inappropriate subjects'. *Alf Layla* employs many of the same journalists who worked for the weekly *al-Doustour*, which was banned in February (*Index* 3/1998). **Ibrahim Issa**, *Alf Layla's* editor-in-chief, said 'the real reason they banned the issue is that they are annoyed that the journalists from *al-Doustour* are back.' (*Cairo Times*, Egyptian Organisation for Human Rights, WAN)

Amr Nassef, a journalist with the opposition daily *al-Arabi*, left jail on 22 August after serving a three-month sentence imposed in May (*Index* 4/1998). (*Cairo Times*)

On 24 August former Interior Minister Hassan al-Alfi dropped his libel suit against **Magdy Hussain**, editor of the fortnightly *al-Shaab*, and reporter **Mohammad Hilal** for exposing abuses of ministerial office for personal gain. The two journalists were jailed in February on one of the charges.

(*Index* 3/1998, 4/1998). Both were released on 3 July when the Court of Cassation overturned the decision of the lower court (*Index* 5/1998) (*Cairo Times*)

On 30 August the Court of Cassation overturned a verdict jailing opposition journalist **Gamal Fahmy**, of the banned weekly *al-Doustour*. Fahmy was sentenced to six months' hard labour by the Appellate Court in March (*Index* 3/1998, 4/1998). Fahmy said on his release: 'This is the first time in 60 years that journalists have been imprisoned, and it's no coincidence it happened now. There are serious suspicions of [government] interference with the lower courts'. (*Cairo Times*)

The grand sheikh of the al-Azhar seminary, Mohammed Sayed Tantawi, filed defamation charges on 8 September against the newspaper *al-Ahrar* for printing an article by **Yehya Ismail**, one of Tantawi's conservative critics and an al-Azhar theology professor. The article accused Tantawi of professional negligence in allowing the US film *The Devil's Advocate*, a 'vehicle for atheism', to be screened in Cairo. (*Cairo Times*)

On 27 September **Hamdy al-Batran**, author of *Diary of a Police Officer in the Countryside*, was suspended from the police service for one month for publishing his novel without permission from the Interior Ministry. In February 1998, al-Batran was demoted from supervisor of police vehicles to maintenance supervisor. His novel is set in Upper Egypt and

gives a first-hand account of an officer caught in the crossfire of extremist violence and official duty. In the book, the officer decides upon early retirement. (*Cairo Times*)

Recent Publications: *Human Rights Abuses by Armed Groups* (AI, September 1998, pp13); *National Reconciliation to Counter Political and Religious Violence* (Group for Democratic Development, September 1998, pp51); *Rightless Women, Heartless Men—Egyptian Women and Domestic Violence* (Legal Research and Resource Centre for Human Rights, 1998, pp109)

ETHIOPIA

Bezunesh Debede, publisher and deputy editor of the Amharic-language weekly *Zegabi*, was arrested on 10 July for unknown reasons and is being held in Maekelawi prison. (RSF)

Exiled journalist **Lulu Kebede** was released unconditionally on 27 August. Kebede had been arrested in Nairobi on 22 August after he and a number of other journalists fled the country. Kebede had been under the protection of the UN High Commission for Refugees and had all his documents in order. (NDIMA)

Four journalists with the defunct weekly *Tobiya* – **Goshu Mogas**, **Biru Tsegaye**, **Anteneh Merid** and **Taye Belachew** – arrested on 16 January were released in late August after seven months in jail (*Index* 2/1998). Tsegaye has been charged and appeared in court in October: the other three have been released without charge. *Tobiya's* premises were destroyed in a mysterious fire hours after the arrests were made. (IFJ)

EUROPEAN UNION

On 21 September it was reported that EU members had decided to step up surveillance on the movements of any 'sizeable groups which may pose a threat to law and order'. Originally set up to monitor football supporters during the 1996 European Championship, the scheme has been extended to include other groups of 'political and social interest', following pressure from the UK government. (*Guardian*)

Between 25 September and 6 October newspapers reported on alleged corruption in the European Commission. Concern centred on the accountability of EU contractors – notably the Luxembourg-based company Perrylux – and £420 million unaccounted for in the commission's humanitarian budget. Humanitarian affairs commissioner Emma Bonino sued the *Financial Times* for defamation over the allegations. In late September, *Libération* reported that Edith Cresson, a former French prime minister who is EU commissioner for research and education, had appointed her former dentist as an AIDS researcher. It was further revealed that, prior to taking up the post, he had worked for Perrylux, an EU contractor for 25 years, hightening fears that the commission had become a haven for nepotism. Cresson attempted unsuccessfully to take out a gagging order in a French court against the *Libération* report. (*Guardian, Daily Telegraph, Financial Times, European*)

FIJI

The Speaker of the House of Representatives attacked the *Fiji Times* on 5 October in calling for action to prevent the publication of government reports prior to their introduction in parliament. Dr. Apenisa Kurisaqila decried the 'arrogant' newspaper for publishing a leaked auditor-general's report that highlighted misuse of public funds in both goverment and military circles. The *Fiji Times* responded in an editorial, saying 'don't blame the messenger'. (PINA)

The government is reviewing the work permits of University of the South Pacific journalism lecturers **David Robie** and **Ingrid Leary**, both New Zealanders. The reviews are in response to accusations that the two breached the terms of their work permits, possibly at the expense of the jobs of local journalists. (PINA)

FRANCE

On 4 September it was reported that the former MI5 officer being held in a Paris jail, **David Shayler**, was being denied access to friends or family. The authorities suggested that the decision resulted from British pressure. Shayler's lawyer, John Wadham, said the ban violated the European Convention on Human Rights. (*Guardian*)

On 5 September French police searched the home of **Claude Ardid** of the daily *Var Matin*, seized documents and detained him in Toulon for 27 hours before eventually levelling a charge of 'violating trial secrecy'. The charge arises from the publication in *Var Matin* in April of a witness's deposition. (RSF)

The 17 Correctional Court of Paris on 11 September fined journalists **Jean-Marie Pontault** and **Jérome Depuis** of the weekly *L'Express* US$1,700, including damages, for 'receiving and publishing investigative secrets'. The charges were brought by Gilles Mènage, former director of President François Mitterand's cabinet, after Pontault and Depuis published transcripts of telephone conversations and minutes of meetings in their book *Les Oreilles du Président*. (RSF)

In early October, following coverage of the Clinton-Lewinsky affair, a group of French doctors issued a Declaration of the Right to Sexual Privacy. Pierre Lavoisier, who drafted the declaration, was shocked at the violation of intimacy and hoped to trigger public debate about politicians 'using people's sexual life as a gun'. (*International Herald Tribune*)

On 7 October judges in Bordeaux prohibited three city libraries from publicly displaying copies of *INRI*, a book of photographs by **Bettina Rheims** which 'explores' the life of Christ.

Father Phillipe Laguerie had denounced the book in the court for the 'wilfull, deliberate and provocative effect' of the cover, which shows a naked and crucified woman. Only one of the libraries obeyed the injunction but another, FNAC, appealed. The success of the ruling will encourage other priests to get the book banned, according to his lawyer Dominique Rémy. (*Le Monde*, *Guardian*)

GABON

On 11 August **Michel Ongoundou-Loundah**, publication director for *La Griffe* newspaper, disappeared from home. He appeared in court in Libreville the following day with the newspaper's editor-in-chief, **Raphael Ntoutoume Nkoghe**, and journalist **Pulchérie Beaumel**. They were charged with criminal libel in connection with a June article which asserted that employees of Air Gabon were involved in ivory trafficking. All three were convicted and sentenced to eight-month prison terms and ordered to pay damages of CFAFr3 million each (approx. US$5,000) to René Morvan, director general of Air Gabon. On 13 August security agents entered *La Griffe's* editorial offices and seized the press cards of all employees. The same day, security agents raided the newspaper's printer and seized 12,000 copies of *La Griffe* along with computer diskettes, thus preventing the sale of the newspaper the following day. (CPJ, RSF)

GAMBIA

The *Daily Observer's* managing director, **Theophilus George**, editor-in-chief **Baba Gale Jallow** and news editor **Dembo Jawo** were detained on 30 August in connection with an article about the discovery of armoured cars and an armoury. They were released two days later.(IFJ)

GEORGIA

Journalist **Amiran Meshkeli** was permitted temporary release from military service at a 17 August hearing. Meshkeli, correspondent for *Orioni*, has been the target of harassment by the defence ministry since he published an interview with soldiers in May 1998. The court found that he had been 'called up in violation of the law'. (Glasnost Defence Foundation)

Lasha Nadareishvili, editor of the independent newspaper *Asaval-Dasavali*, and correpondent **David Okropiridze** were severely beaten on the night of 10 September by a group of armed men. The newspaper has criticised figures from both the government and the opposition. (CPJ, *Droni*)

Journalists **Kote Vardzelashvili** and **Gogi Kavtaradze**, who work for the non-governmental Liberty Institute, were badly beaten and threatened by Tbilisi police on 23 September as they attempted to interview city Police Chief Mgebrishvili. The journalists were forced into a car and taken to a police station, where they were detained for two hours. (RSF)

Recent Publication: *Summary of Amnesty International's Concerns* (AI, August 1998, 30pp)

GERMANY

On 25 August Chancellor Helmut Kohl rejected the findings of a study into child poverty. The study, carried out by an independent body and commissioned by the government, concluded that one in nine children living in former West Germany relied on state handouts for their survival. In the east, the figure was as high as one in five. (Reuters)

GHANA

A publisher facing criminal libel charges died on 21 September as he was about to appear in court for a story alleging that the government had dealt cocaine in order to finance arms purchases. The death of **Tommy Thompson**, publisher of the *Ghana Free Press*, was announced in court by his lawyer and the case was immediately adjourned. He had been charged together with **Nana Kofi Coomson,** editor of the *Ghanaian Chronicle*, for publishing the same allegations. (Free Expression Ghana)

GREECE

On 18 August Justice Minister Evangelos Yannopoulos proposed the expansion of slander and libel laws to include a minimum two-year sentence for journalists and news editors, who insult politicians or members of public in the broadcast media. Yannopoulos then announced he would bring charges of aggravated defamation against the right-wing newspaper *Eleftheros Typos* for an editorial critical of the government in its 17 August edition. (International Press Institute)

On 2 September **Abdulahim Dede**, a journalist from the Turkish minority, was sentenced to eight months in prison for trying to install a radio antenna in his back yard. He was arrested the previous day under the expeditious procedure, which is chiefly used for building without a permit. (Greek Helsinki Monitor)

On 17 September the journalist **Makis Triantafyllopoulos** was convicted and sentenced to an eight-month suspended sentence for defaming Justice Minister Yannopoulos. His article in the daily *Kalimera* accused the minister of interfering with justice in the case implicating the governor of the Social Security Fund, Gregory Solomos. (Greek Helsinki Monitor)

On 21 September the three-member Misdemeanour Court of Salonica sentenced *Avriani* newspaper publisher **George Kouris**, editor **George Tsiroyannis** and journalist **Stelios Vorinas** to four years and 11 months in prison. They were convicted of the aggravated defamation and insult of Yannis Raptopoulos, owner of the rival publications *Salonica* and *Thessaloniki*.

On 22 September a Macedonian Television (MTV) crew was refused entry visas by the Liaison Office in Skopje. They intended to cover the trial of members of the Macedonian minority party Rainbow, who were later acquitted of the charge of 'using their mother tongue'. (Greek Helsinki Monitor)

INDIA

On 20 August Communications Minister Sushma Swaraj was reported to have banned access to international telephone sex lines, describing the service as immoral and a drain on foreign exchange. (BBC World Service)

In mid-September police in the northern state of Himachal Pradesh arrested two Tibetans at Dharamsala, following a tip-off they had been sent by China to monitor the movements of the Dalai Lama. The arrests followed reports of a plot to assassinate the exiled Tibetan spiritual leader. (BBC World Service)

INDONESIA

After more than four years of enforced closure, *Tempo* relaunched on 6 October. The magazine, which once had a circulation of 180,000, was shut down on 21 June 1994 (*Index* 4/5/1994, 6/1994, 1/1995, 3/1995, 4/1995, 1/1996, 4/1996, 6/1996). (ISAI)

On 30 September, journalist **Rudy Goenawan** was summoned to appear at police headquarters on 1 October, in connection with an article he wrote in the publication *Jakarta Jakarta*, alleging that a woman was raped by a group of men who told her that 'she must be raped', because she was Chinese. (CPJ)

IRAQ

Journalist **Dawoud al-Farhan** of the Cairo-based Middle East News Agency was arrested in Baghdad in July and taken to the Ministry of Information. Efforts to determine the place of his detention failed. Al-Farhan was released on 8 October without explanation. (Associated Press)

The Centre for Human Rights of the Iraqi Communist Party released a report in August on the mass execution in Abu Ghraib prison of 62 detainees who had been held since the Kurdish revolt of 1991. The executions were part of the government's 'Clean Up Prisons Campaign', initiated last year. (Iraq Foundation)

IRAN

Mohammed Reza Zaeri, publisher of *Khaneh*, was arrested on 29 July and released on bail for publishing an anonymous letter criticising the late Ayatollah Khomeini for being responsible for the deaths of hundreds of thousands of youths during the Iran-Iraq war and causing Iran's international isolation by issuing a *fatwa* against writer Salman Rushdie (*Index* 5/1998). On 6 August *Khaneh*'s licence was permanently revoked; Zaeri was fined US$1,700; and he was given a six-month suspended sentence. Other recently banned publications including *Gozaresh-e Rouz, Rah-e Nouand* and *Tavana*. (RSF)

On 1 August the offices of the publication *Aftab'e Emrooz/Tous*, were stormed and

SUBSCRIBE & SAVE

UK and overseas

○ **Yes! I want to subscribe to *Index*.**

❐ 1 year (6 issues)   £39   Save 28%
❐ 2 years (12 issues)   £74   Save 31%
❐ 3 years (18 issues)   £102   **You save 37%**

Name

Address

                                                                    B8B6

£ _____ enclosed. ❏ Cheque (£) ❏ Visa/MC ❏ Am Ex ❏ Bill me
(*Outside of the UK, add £6 a year for foreign postage*)

Card No.

Expiry   Signature

❏ I do not wish to receive mail from other companies.

✉ Freepost: INDEX, 33 Islington High Street, London N1 9BR
☎ (44) 171 278 2313   Fax: (44) 171 278 1878
e syra@indexoncensorship.org

SUBSCRIBE & SAVE

North America

○ **Yes! I want to subscribe to *Index*.**

❐ 1 year (6 issues) $52   Save 21%
❐ 2 years (12 issues) $96   Save 27%
❐ 3 years (18 issues) $135   **You save 32%**

Name

Address

                                                                    B8B6

$ _____ enclosed. ❏ Cheque ($) ❏ Visa/MC ❏ Am Ex ❏ Bill me

Card No.

Expiry   Signature

❏ I do not wish to receive mail from other companies.

✉ INDEX, 708 Third Avenue, 8th Floor, New York, NY 10017
☎ (44) 171 278 2313   Fax: (44) 171 278 1878
e syra@indexoncensorship.org

an editor **Mahmoud Shams**, and two Associated Press reporters, **Afshin Valinejad** and **Anwatr Faruqi**, were assaulted. (*About Iran*)

It was reported on 6 August that **Hamid Reza Jalali-Pour**, proprietor of *Jameah* newspaper, closed down by the authorities in June (*Index 5/1998*), received a suspended five-year sentence for 'publishing lies, insulting state authorities and distorting the utterances of deceased spiritual leader Ayatollah Khomenei'. (BBC World Service)

Moshen Said-Zadeh, a clergy writer who advocates more equality for women, has been in detention since 21 June, according to a report on 27 August. (*About Iran*) **Mashallah Shamsol-va-Ezine**, editor of the banned Iranian daily *Tous*, publishing director **Hamid Reza Jalei-Pour**, sub-editor **Mohammed Javadi-Hessar** and journalist **Ebrahim Nabavi** were arrested on 16 September by revolutionary guards who occupied and sealed the paper's offices. They face charges of 'subversive activities', which can invoke the death penalty, if found guilty. *Tous*, launched with many of the same journalists as *Jameah* which was was banned in June, criticised Ayatollah Ali Khamanei for the build-up up military tension along the border with Afghanistan. *Tous* was also banned on 1 August by the Tehran Justice Department (*Index 5/1998*). (RSF)

Abbas Amir-Entezam, pro-democracy leader and winner of a 1997 International Human Rights award, was arrested on charges of defamation on 8 September following remarks he made about revolutionary warden and prosecutor Assadollah Lajaevardi, who had been assassinated by members of Iraq-based *Mujahedin Khalq* organisation a fortnight earlier. (*About Iran*)

Taliban sources announced on 11 September that 'independent' fighters had killed IRNA journalist **Mahmoud Saremi** along with 10 Iranian diplomats after the movement's successful attack on Mazar-i-Sharif in the first week of August. (IPI)

Two journalists with press agency IRNA were freed on bail worth US$33,333 on 23 September, a day after being arrested for publishing news of an early-September assassination attempt on the director of the foundation which oversees welfare payments to victims of the Iran-Iraq war. The arrested are named as deputy managing director **Mohammed Reza Sadeq** and social affairs editor **Ali Reza Khosravi**. (RSF)

The intellectual monthly *Jamah Salem* was banned by a court in Tehran on 29 September after being found guilty of misrepresenting the utterances of the late Ayatollah Khomenei. Director **Siavoch Gouran** was given a one-year suspended sentence and fined US$1,000. (RSF)

Nude works by Renoir, Monet and Pissarro in a collection owned by the state may soon be displayed at the Museum for Contemporary Art after the Ministry of Culture Guidance granted for an exhibition on (*International Herald Trib.*)

It was reported on 8 October that **Mohammed Salamat** director of radical weekly *Asre-è-Ma*, was jailed for publishing 'insulting and deceitful' articles, fined $1,000 and suspended from publishing for six months. **Mehdi Nassiri**, director of the hard-line *Sobh*, was fined $1,000 and suspended for four months. (RSF)

IRELAND

On 29 September the Department of Justice announced that publications aimed at the 'youth market' were to be included in the first fundamental review of censorship laws since the 1920s. Youth Affairs Minister Willie O'Dea welcomed the announcement. 'Many of these publications,' he said, 'are countering the good work being done by health promotion units and various drug awareness organisations.' (*Irish Independent*)

ITALY

Fr Leonardo Zega, a leading Roman Catholic liberal and former editor of the Catholic weekly *Famiglia Christiana*, called for a more open approach to pornography on 16 September, saying it was morally acceptable for couples with 'problems' to reinforce relationships by watching pornographic films, especially where this would 'contribute to conjugal complicity between husband and wife'. (*The Times*)

JAPAN

...sa Nakatsu, Beijing
...pondent for the Japanese
...y *Yomiuri Shimbum*, was
...eported from China on 6
October. Officials said that he
'stole state secrets', but
colleagues say the real motive
for his expulsion was his links
with journalist **Shi Binhai**,
who was arrested on 5
September. (RSF)

JORDAN

On 8 August **Nahed Hattar**,
editor-in-chief of the critical
opposition weekly *al-Mithaq*,
was beaten unconscious by four
unidentified attackers as he got
out of his car at his home in
Jabal Hussein. (CPJ, *Middle East
International*)

Hussein Emoush, editor-in-
chief of the satirical weekly
Abed Rabbo, was arrested in the
middle of the night on 10
August by a group of more than
10 police officers. Emoush had
written articles critical of the
water-pollution crisis and the
government's new press laws.
(RSF)

KAZAKHSTAN

The authorities were preparing
in early September to expel six
Pakistanis allegedly engaged in
spreading Wahabbi propaganda.
The National Security
Committee detained the men
after being tipped off that they
would attend a Muslim
conference in the Jambyl
Region. (Interfax)

The Almaty office of the
independent Russian-language
weekly *XXI Vek* (21st Century)

was destroyed by two petrol
bombs in the early hours of 26
September. Police sealed off the
premises, refusing editor
Bigeldy Gabdullin and his
staff entry. On 28 September,
the paper's parent company was
told to close by the Almaty City
Juridical Board. No explanation
was given and editorial staff
have appealed to the Almaty
City Court. *XXI Vek* regularly
published materials criticising
the Kazakh leadership,
including the opinions of
former prime minister Akejan
Kazhegeldin. Earlier in
September, a private printing
house and the state distribution
company tore up contracts with
XXI Vek, forcing the last three
issues to be printed outside the
country. (Glasnost Defence
Foundation, RFE/RL, CPJ,
RSF)

KENYA

A guard working for the *Star*
newspaper was arrested by
plainclothes policemen on 29
July. The arrest followed an
attempt to impound copies of
the paper which failed after
intervention by staff and
members of the public. The
man was later released without
charge. (NDIMA, 31 July)

Two Nairobi journalists facing
charges of producing a
publication without executing a
publisher's bond were denied
bail on 10 September and
remained in custody until 16
September. **George Nakhoshi
Wamalwa** and **Tom Oscar
Alwaka** first appeared before a
magistrate on 9 July. The two
denied irregularly publishing
the *Kenya Dispatch* between 7
and 13 September 1998.

(NDIMA)

East African Standard
correspondant **Waiyengera
Abuyeka** was abducted by a
medical doctor who took
offence to an article filed by the
correspondent. It was reported
on 8 September that the doctor
beat Abuyeka, threatening to
inject him with HIV after he
wrote about the doctor's wife
being discovered in bed with
another man. (NDIMA)

KUWAIT

On 18 August 40 men from the
Salab tribe ransacked the offices
of daily *Al-Qabas* in Kuwait
City in response to the
republication of a 1940s picture
showing Salab women dancing
without veils in front of men.
The caption explained that the
Salab acted this way because
they are 'a mix of Arabs and
other peoples who came to
Islam later'. In June editor-in-
chief **Mohammed Jassem al-
Saqr** was sentenced to six
months in jail. (RSF)

KYRGYZSTAN

On 18 August the weekly *Asaba*
was evicted from the building
that has housed it for nearly 60
years. The Interior Ministry,
which now owns the building,
disregarded a 15 August
demonstration by 500 people in
Bishkek's central square.
Ownership was transferred to
the ministry in 1991, but
former Prime Minister Apas
Jumagulov had allowed *Asaba*,
now an opposition newspaper,
to continue there. (Bureau on
Human Rights and Rule of
Law, RFE/RL)

Non-government TV and radio stations were given 10 days from 19 August to increase the proportion of Kyrgyz-language programming. On 3 September, the NAC informed broadcasters that it would charge them for the cost of supervising their mandatory licensing agreements. (Bureau on Human Rights and Rule of Law)

Vecherny Bishkek reporter **Rina Prijivoyt** criticised local journalists in a 21 August article for 'blindly repeating' the public relations message of the Kumtor Operating Company (KOC), the Canadian-owned gold producer at the centre of a poisoning incident which allegedly cause the deaths of several villagers. Prijivoyt wrote that the large sums that KOC has since spent on media 'engagement' had succeeded in getting concern about the spillage portrayed in local media as 'hysteria'. (Bureau on Human Rights and Rule of Law)

Bishkek's Leninsky Regional Court opened a hearing on 21 September into alleged 'rude insinuations and defamation' of parliamentarian Ishenbay Kadyrbekov by journalist **Kalen Sydykova**. Sydykova wrote a piece titled 'Parliamentary Crime or Ventures of Presumptuous MPs' for the 11 June edition of the newspaper *Kylmysh Jana Jaza* ('Crime and Punishment'). Kadyrbekov is seeking US$50,000 as compensation for 'harm to his dignity and honour'. (Bureau on Human Rights and Rule of Law)

Rustam Koshmuratov, founder of the Almaz radio

station, went to court in late September to challenge the National Communications Agency's (NCA) decision to annul the station's agreements with western broadcasters. The NCA claimed that the recent appointment of a new director invalidated agreements with stations such as Radio Liberty and Deutsche Welle that named the station director as Koshmuratov. The NAC closed Radio Almaz temporarily in late February 1990 (*Index* 3/1998, 4/1998) (Bureau on Human Rights and Rule of Law)

LESOTHO

Several journalists covering the upheaval that engulfed the tiny state in September were seriously injured, as soldiers or mobs turned on them. On 22 September, freelance photographer **Greg Marinovich** was shot in the leg while covering the unrest. Unknown assailants attacked **Johannes Sefatsa**, a cameraman with the South African Broadcasting Corporation, leaving him seriously wounded. Later in the day an Associated Press (AP) correspondent and photographer and a BBC cameraman were attacked by a stone-throwing mob. They abandoned their car an hour later when it was raked with gunfire by Basotho soldiers. The same day two AP Television cameramen were hijacked and another mob threw a rock through the window of a car driven by *Guardian* reporter **Alex Duval Smith**. On 23 September **Sam Kiley**, correspondent for *Time*,

was wounded by gunfire. (MISA

LIBYA

At least 33 scientists, university lecturers and medical doctors were arrested in a countrywide swoop in June by security police. The arrests came at a time when professional bodies are becoming increasingly strident in opposition to government policies. Those arrested were dubbed sympathisers of the Libyan Islamic Group, a non-violent Islamist movement. (AAASHRAN)

MALAWI

On 18 September, government banned an opposition weekly newspaper, the *National Agenda,* saying that the directors of Chikonzero Publications, its publisher, had registered false names to obtain its licence. A government statement broadcast on Malawi Radio said: 'It will be unlawful from now onwards for any person, company or institution to publish, print or circulate the *National Agenda* in this country.' The weekly had angered the authorities by reporting on scandals, corruption and human rights violations since its inception four months ago. (RSF, Panafrican News Agency)

Dingi Chirwa, editor of the private *New Vision* newspaper, was arrested and beaten by police before being released on bail. He had published an article, 'Nine Bombs Found in Lilongwe' which, police said, contained false information that could lead to a breach of the peace. In the same month, **Bright Sonani**, a reporter with the *Daily Times*, was threatened with death by four men as he was taking pictures of a university graduation ceremony in Zomba. The men threatened to beat him up because he was 'fond of writing stupid stories about the president'. (RSF)

On 5 October police arrested prominent politician **Brian Mungomo,** whom they suspect to be behind the banned weekly *National Agenda*. Mungomo, who writes a column in the independent *Daily Times*, told a reporter: 'I knew they would arrest me one day, because any person critical of the government is being taken as an alien in this country. (Panafrican News Agency)

Information Minister Sam Mpasu in October banned *Take Part,* a newsletter for civic education published by the NGO German Technical Coorperation (GTZ). In a letter to the management, Mpasu said that 'non-governmental organisations were not allowed to publish newspapers in the country'. (All Africa News Agency)

MALAYSIA

On 9 August Information Minister Mohamed Rahmat announced that he planned to impose restrictions that will allow the government to monitor more closely the movements of foreign journalists. (CPJ)

After an investigation of internet providers, two unnamed Malaysians were

arrested under the Internal Security Act on 12 August for allegedly 'spreading rumours' of riots through a news group. (*Independent*)

On 2 September deputy prime minister and finance minister **Anwar Ibrahim** was removed from the party after accusations of sexual misconduct and sodomy, which are illegal. On 20 September Ibrahim was arrested under the Internal Security Act, which provides for indefinite detention without trial. Police kicked down the door of his house, gave him an hour to pack, eat his dinner and say goodbye to his family before driving him away in a white van. (*Guardian, International Herald Tribune*)

MEXICO

Venancio Hernández Hernández, president of a regional branch of the Mexican League for the Defence of Human Rights, was detained in the street by two policemen on 18 July and asked to sign a blank sheet of paper. When he refused, he was threatened with death. (Observatory)

On 10 August the newspaper *México Hoy* published an article accusing **Angelica Ayala Ortiz,** vice-president of the Mexican League of Human Rights, of being a member of the political wing of an armed group. Another human rights activist, **David Fernandez**, has been accused of being responsible for the training of guerrillas. The accusations are part of a defamation campaign by government and its media allies. (Observatory)

On 29 August physicist **Bernardo Salas** released a report about his dismissal from the Central Laguna Verde nuclear plant. Salas lost his 11-year position as coordinator of the radiological protection team when he denounced irregularities at the power station. (AASHRAN)

NAMIBIA

President Sam Nujoma, and Home Affairs Minister Jerry Ekandjo have served separate summonses on the weekly *Windhoek Observer* for defamation and are demanding a total of up to US$200,000 in damages. President Nujoma served his summons against editor **Hannes Smith** on 7 August and is demanding NR1 million for a series of articles that accused him of abuse of office, nepotism, criminal conduct, corruption and homosexual activities. President Nujoma said 'he has been injured in his good name and reputation in his feelings and dignity in general.' Ekandjo's complaint arises from an article which implied that he had abused his position to subvert the rule of law and that he was engaged in corrupt practices. No court dates have been set in either case. Smith said he will defend both cases 'to the bitter end.' In February Smith was sentenced to four months in prison for contempt of court (*Index* 2/1998). ((MISA)

The Namibia Broadcasting Corporation (NBC) has dropped its popular daily morning *Press Review* programme for the second time in eight months. On 7 October the *Namibian* newspaper quoted NBC Director General Ben Mulongeni as saying the programme had been axed to create more time for local news and that there was 'no time for it anywhere else.' The National Society for Human Rights (NSHR) criticised the decision, saying it was 'purely political'. (MISA)

NIGERIA

On 13 August four journalists were beaten and chased away by military security officers at the Benue state government house. **Joyce Bur**, Benue state correspondant for *New Nigeria*, **John Babajide** of the *Tribune*, **Onah Ogun** of *Champion* and **Sunday Orinya** of the *News* and *Tempo* magazines, were beaten with horse whips when they tried to get into the banquet hall to cover a hand-over ceremony of military administrators. ('IPR')

Okenzie Amaruben, journalist and publisher of the Enugu quarterly *Newsservice*, was shot dead by a policeman on 28 August. Amaruben had gone to check on a job at his printer's workshop. He found the policeman waiting for the printer, whom he had come to arrest after a complaint by a female client. In his absence, the police decided to arrest his staff. When Amaruben tried to intervene, the policeman hit him on the head with the muzzle of the gun, shouting at him to go into a waiting police vehicle. In the vehicle, there was a deafening noise. The policeman has since been arrested. ('IPR')

Moshood Fayemiwo, publisher and editor-in-chief of the defunct weekly tabloid *Razor*, was released from detention on 2 September. Fayemiwo was kidnapped by government agents in Cotonou, Benin, where he had sought temporary asylum. He has been detained at the Directorate of Military Intelligence in Lagos since 14 February 1997. No reasons for his abduction were given. ('IPR')

A group of Ogoni activists, imprisoned with the executed writer **Ken Saro-Wiwa** and held since 1994 on charges of murdering four pro-government chiefs, were freed unconditionally on 8 September. (*Guardian*)

PAKISTAN

On 16 August 12 members of the youth wing of the Pakistan Muslim League (PML) attacked **Khawaja Danial Salim**, editor-in-chief of a weekly, in the Chakwal city press club for publishing an allegedly anti-PML story. Salim was saved from serious harm by other media workers. (Pakistan Press Foundation)

Asif Khokar, chief editor of the daily *Insaf*, **Basar Khokar**, bureau chief of the daily *Insaf*, and **Ch. Yaseen Saleemi**, a Pakistan Press International correspondent, were fired upon on 17 August by the accused in a gang rape that they had written about. (Pakistan Press Foundation)

On 28 August Prime Minister Nawaz Sharif introduced a constitutional amendment to replace British common law with laws based on the Koran and Sunna, the traditions of Islam. The amendment was passed by the lower house of parliament in early October, but opposition parties have vowed to block the amendment in the Senate. (Associated Press, Reuters)

In early September it was reported that **Zafaryab Ahmed**, a columnist and human rights activist, was not being allowed to make use of a teaching fellowship at Colby College, Maine, because his name continues to be on the Exit Control List (ECL). Ahmed was charged with anti-state activities after his campaign against child labour led to a reduction in carpet exports. (CPJ, Pakistan Press Foundation)

On 9 September the Shia **Ghulam Akbar** was sentenced to death for blaspheming the Prophet Mohammed. Akbar was first arrested in 1995, although the exact details of his alleged offence are not known because to specify them could, in itself, be a legal offence. Akbar is the first Muslim to be sentenced under the blasphemy law which is usually used against Christians (*Index* 4/1998). (BBC World Service, *The Times*)

On 15 September **Pervaiz ul Hassan**, a journalist working in Azad Jammu and Kashmir, was arrested after reporting on corruption in the police force and civil administration. (Pakistan Press Foundation)

On 26 September **Saeed Iqbal**

WOLE SOYINKA

Nigerian digest

' The following morality tale must be familiar to many. It speaks directly to the dilemma that confronts Nigeria. The tale goes thus: The various parts of the body once rebelled against the Stomach, complaining that it was an idle, bloated guzzler of the good things of life, while others slaved to keep the body functioning. I do all the thinking, said the Head, my eyes seek out nature and warn of danger, directing the limbs in their productive labour. The Arm, of course, pointed to its muscular wear-and-tear in the service of the Body, while the Legs reminded the others that, but for their joint function as the Ministry of Transport, Body would simply stay and rot in one spot. Shoulders, Buttocks, Spinal Column etc, all joined in iterating their responsibility to the general well-being of the Body, except Stomach, who could hardly deny that the food always made its way to his storage tanks. Stomach maintained a dignified silence. Finally the parts decided to go on strike and starve Stomach to death.

The rest of the tale is easily imagined. Stomach warned that it was merely the Ministry of Supplies and Distribution, that what it received through Mouth and Throat went back to the rest of the Body. The strike began and, of course, all the body parts began to atrophy, Stomach outlasting them all. As with all good morality tales with a happy ending, they all came to their senses before too much damage was done and Stomach resumed its revered place in the structure of things.

I would like to say that whoever thought of this morality tale had never stepped foot into Nigeria ... Within our space, it surely is a clear case of 'monkey dey work, baboon dey chop' and baboon, in this case, is very definitely the Stomach, placed at the centre of things, guzzling away at the products of the Head, Arms, Legs Shoulders and Spine, and redistributing – nothing. Or else a mere pittance.'

Nobel laureate **Wole Soyinka** *returned to Nigeria on 14 October after four years in exile. Two days later, he spoke at length in Lagos about the need to 're-design' the relations between the constituent parts of the nation if its democratic aspirations are to be met. This is an edited extract.*

Hashmi, chief reporter for the daily *Mashriq*'s bureau in Peshawar, went into hiding when he received death threats and a *fatwa* was reportedly issued against him by local clerics. The threats seem to be linked to a 14 September article in which Hashmi reported an increase in child abuse at various religious seminaries, and another in which he linked the general secretary of the *Jamiat-i-Ulema-i-Islam* (JUI) with building irregularities in North West Frontier Province. The JUI is a backer of Afghanistan's Taliban movement. (RSF)

Members of the religious group *Tehrik e Jafaria Pakistan* (TJP) attacked four photojournalists in Karachi on 27 September. The journalists – **Shoaib Ahmad** of *Jang*, **Riaz Shamid** of *Ibrat*, **Javed Jeayja** of *Kawish* and **Ashraf Momson** of *Quumi Akhbar* – had been covering the funeral of a slain TJP leader and his son. (Pakistan Press Foundation)

On 30 September and 1 October Special Branch officers entered the offices of the monthly *Newsline* and badgered employees for the telephone numbers and home addresses of the editorial staff. The police were ostensibly investigating the magazine's tax irregularities, but editor **Rehana Hakim** believes that they were sent to harass him because of a series of articles in *Newsline* on financial irregularities by Prime Minister Sharif, his family and associates. (Pakistan Press Foundation, *Dawn*)

PALESTINE

On 18 August **Abdullah al-Shami**, a contributor to the Islamist weekly *al-Istiqlal*, was detained without warrant at his home in al-Shujaeyyah by officers from the Criminal Investigation Unit. The detention followed a 14 August article critical of the newly formed cabinet, which alleged rampant corruption in the government of President Arafat. Al-Shami has been denied access to attorney and his current whereabouts are not known. (CPJ)

On 13 September **Saber Noureddine**, an Agence France Presse photojournalist in Gaza, was arrested and detained for 10 hours by police officers on suspicion of being a member of the Hamas Islamic Movement. The previous day, police had confiscated his camera and personal ID card while he was photographing a Hamas demonstration (RSF)

PAPUA NEW GUINEA

The Censorship Board has lifted the December 1991 prohibition of *Cosmopolitan* and *Cleo*, which suppressed the magazines on the grounds that they contained nudity and 'advertisements for sex-aids'. The board's chairman said on 28 September that the magazines contain 'helpful articles' and that they will be available again for sale to adults only. (PINA)

Journalists were escorted into a guarded Port Moresby courtroom on 23 August to report on a woman who was videotaped having sex with a prominent politician – four days after police blocked journalists from attending the same case. The woman faces a charge under the Classification of Publication Censorship Act. (PINA)

PARAGUAY

On 20 August journalists were prevented from covering the ceremony in which authority was handed over to a new commander of the 'National Armada'. The press was also prohibited from covering the meeting of the foreign minister with US Ambassador Maura Harty or obtaining interviews with Interior Minister Ruben Arias Mandoza. (Paraguay Union of Journalists)

On 21 August journalist **Jose Rojas** from Channel 9 received blows from security officials attempting to prevent him from interviewing the Minister of Public Works, Victor Segovia Rios as he left a government office. (Paraguay Union of Journalists)

On 24 August members of the Paraguay Union of Journalists demonstrated outside Government Palace in protest at increased restrictions on freedom of expression, as well as intimidation of journalists, since the government of Cubas Grau which assumed power on 15 August. (Paraguay Union of Journalists)

PERU

On 21 August public prosecutor Jose Ochoa Lamas began a criminal investigation against journalist **Cesar Hildebrandt**

Perez prompted by a complaint filed by Santiago Sanguinetti. The complaint, based on the broadcast of allegedly confidential information on the Channel 13 television news programme *En Persona*, concerned details given by Foreign Affairs Minister Eduardo Ferrero Costa in a closed session of Congress about the incursion of 300 Ecuadorian troops into Peruvian territory. Sanguinetti claims that the broadcast was an offence against national security and constituted treason. (IPYS)

Jose Olaya, editor-in-chief of the Lima daily *El Tio*, received on 25 August an anonymous telephone call in which a caller shouted: 'This time they won't miss'. Two years ago, two assailants on a motorcycle shot at him seven times at point-blank range while travelling in his car with his wife. At that time Olaya was working for the daily *El Chino*. (IPYS)

After serving one-third of his five-year sentence, general manager of Radio Miraflores **Ricardo Palma Michelsen** was freed on 27 August. Palma was serving a term at San Jorge prison for tax evasion. (IPYS)

On 8 September the Supreme Court annulled the 23 January verdict by the Puno Superior Court which absolved six army officers and one civilian tried for the bombing of Radio Samoa and Channel 13-Global Television in October 1996. The Supreme Court has allowed 30 days for further investigations before a new trial takes place. (IPYS)

The trial against **Baruch Ivcher** on charges of customs fraud, tax evasion and falsifying documents began on 14 September (*Index* 4/1997, 5/1997, 6/1997, 2/1998, 3/1998, 4/1998, 5/1998). The prosecutor is demanding a 12-year prison term. (IPYS)

Journalist **Isaac García Villanueva** has been target of a defamation campaign since 27 September in the shape of advertisements, articles and editorials accusing him of treason. There is a fear that he could also become target of physical attack. (IPYS)

ROMANIA

Florentin Florescu and **Dragos Stangu** of the independent daily *Monitorul*, were fined 100 million lei (US$11,250) after being convicted of libel on 29 August. for accusing a local politician of abusing his position by quashing court proceedings against his son. Two days later **Cornel Sabou**, a journalist from *Baia Mare*, began serving as 10-month sentence for libel. Convicted in April, Sabou was fined 500,000 lei (US$57) and ordered pay 300 million lei in damages for articles accusing a local judge of forgery. (RSF, RFE/RL)

On 9 September the government ordered that legal action be taken against the publishers of the weekly *Atac la persoana* after it published an article regretting the lack of 'barbed wire and Cyclone-B gas' to 'deal with' the Jews. (RFE/RL)

RUSSIA

On 14 August **Sergei Fufayev** was assaulted by three unidentified men in the Bashkortostan city of Ufa. Fufayev, a reporter and regular critic of the authorities for the independent *Otechestvo*, believed the attack was politically motivated as he was told by his attackers to 'get away' from the region. (RFE/RL, Glasnost Defence Foundation)

On 24 August, four days after suffering serious head injuries in an attack outside his house in St Petersburg, **Anatoly Levin-Utkin**, deputy editor-in-chief of *Yuridichesky Peterburg Segodnya*, died without regaining consciousness. Levin-Utkin was found unconscious and his briefcase, containing material for the paper's next issue and photo equipment, was missing. *Yuridichesky Peterburg Segodnya* had recently published articles on corruption in St Petersburg's banking circles. (Glasnost Defence Foundation)

Six years after his death, ballet dancer **Rudolf Nuryev** was posthumously rehabilitated on 21 September. The prosecutor-general could find no evidence to support his 1962 conviction for high treason. (RFE/RL)

SAMOA

On 16 September the Supreme Court ordered *Samoa Observer* editor-publisher **Savea Sano Malifa** to pay £23,000 in costs over a defamation case brought against him by Prime Minister Tofilau Eti Alesana (*Index* 4/1997, 5/1997, 6/1997, 1/1998, 3/1998, 4/1998). But the court decided that Malifa had been successful in his main argument that recent New Zealand legal precedents on qualified privilege for statements about current, former or aspiring politicians should also apply in Samoa. The argument was opposed by the Australian Queen's Counsel representing Tofilau, whose legal expenses were paid from public funds. Malifa and the *Observer* have already been forced to pay £15,000 in the defamation judgement, but this latest award was a far cry from the £165,000 Tofilau had sought. (PINA)

SERBIA-MONTENEGRO

On 12 August authorities declared veteran Balkan correspondant **Erich Rathfelder** *persona non grata* and ordered him to leave the country, after he wrote in the Berlin daily *taz*, and Vienna's *Die Presse*, that government forces had buried hundreds of ethnic Albanian corpses in mass graves in Rahovec. EU monitors were unable to confirm his report, but Rathfelder and his editors stand by the story. (RFE/RL)

On 14 August **Friedhelm Brebeck** and two cameramen, all journalists for the German public television channel ARD, were expelled from Kosovo after the authorities officially accused them of encouraging ethnic Albanians to set fire to a house in Junik to film the incident. Two days later German Foreign Minister Klaus Kinkel warned authorities that Yugoslav journalists in Bonn might face problems if Brebeck was not

readmitted. (RFE/RL)

On 18 August City Radio in Nis ceased broadcasting after two policemen and inspectors from the Telecommunications Ministry entered the studios, banned its operation and seized part of its transmitter. (AMARC, ANEM)

Five days after last being seen in the city of Orahovac, Kosovo on 21 August, Radio Pristina journalist **Djuro Slavuj** and his driver **Ranko Perinic** were feared abducted by members of the Kosovo Liberation Army. They are the first Serbs in the media to have been reported missing during the six-month conflict. The following day **Musa Kurhasku**, correspondent for the Albanian-language daily *Koha Ditor*, was detained for seven hours, beaten and later released. (HRW, RSF, CPJ)

On 1 September the director general of Radio-Television Serbia (RTS), Dragoljub Milanovic, told the independent Radio B92 to remove its transmitter from the RTS facility by 1 November. The transmitter is RTS property and B92 staff have neither rights nor access to it. The following day Milanovic sent a similar request to Belgrade based Radio Index (*Index* 5/1998), thereby contravening a contract that allows the station to use RTS facilities. Radio Index requested the allocation of a frequency from the Federal Minister of Telecommunications earlier this year, but has not yet received a response. (RSF)

On 17 September the Negotin

Municipality building inspection effected an earlier order to remove parts of STV Negotin radio station's antennae. According to ANEM the authorities actions were illegal and indicated their desire to silence a voice providing objective information with an impartial editorial policy. (ANEM)

One month prior to ANEM's international conference, 'Broadcasting for a Democratic Europe', which was to have been held in Belgrade on 2-3 October, Radio B92 informed the Foreign Ministry and requested that all foreign invitees be issued with visas without hindrance. Three days before the event, ANEM learnt that many foreign participants, including top Council of Europe officials, had been denied visas. The authorities' actions imposed, in effect, a *de facto* ban and the event was cancelled. (ANEM)

As the crisis over Kosovo led to threats of NATO air strikes in early October, government officials warned of reprisals against the independent media. In a reference to journalists, Deputy Prime Minister Vojislav Seselj said: 'We can't shoot down every NATO plane, but we can grab those agents who are at hand'. He was supported by the Prime Minister Mirko Marjanovic, who accused the media of 'spreading lies and fear', and MP Zeljko Simic, who charged journalists with 'high treason' for reporting the conflict. The attack was picked up by the Information Ministry on 5 October, when it called upon all media that rebroadcast

ALEKSANDR VUCIS

Voice of Serbia

We admit we are thrilled by your concern that the Serbian media can be organised in a better way than under Serbian law. But, believe us, we are a little surprised by the double standards to which you resort in the fight to establish alleged democratic relations in all parts of the world.

You say you condemn the 'draconian' law on public information adopted by the National Assembly of Serbia, but we remember that you never condemned the dreadful sanctions imposed on Yugoslavia by the countries from which you most frequently write. You never condemned the killing of civilians in *Republika Srpska* and you never condemned the fact that, because of your democratic bombs charged with who knows what, Serbian women still give birth to sick children even today.

Serbian norms on responsible information are similar to those in the countries from which the worst accusations against us have come – with the exception that fines for violation are not nearly as steep. We have made a mistake here, we admit it.

Do you regard as 'independent' media those whose editing policy is most frequently directed against the interests of our country, which do not depend on our country but on yours? An odd term, isn't it? In one letter you say that these media are banned, although they still openly speak about alleged Serbian oppression in [Kosovo] and about alleged Serbian capitulation.

Like you, we are determined to promote open media in the world. In Serbia, there are over 2,500 registered public media with the right to inform the public without censorship or pressure from the state. You boast you have stepped up Serbian broadcasts on the Voice of America and BBC, but rest assured that we shall soon boast of stronger signals and more extensive English programming on Radio Yugoslavia, Serbian Radio, TV and other media.

As enthusiasts of the flow of free information throughout the world, we are certain that you will help us in our goal to inform the citizens of your countries in the simplest possible way about everything that is happening in our country.

Aleksandr Vucis is Serbia's Information Minister. In response to the many letters of reproach from international organisations, institutions and NGOs concerned with media freedom under President Slobodan Milosevic, this edited statement was issued in late October.

programmes produced by 'services for the propaganda and psychological war of western powers', to cease doing so. (RTS)

On 5 October **Sulejman Klokoqi**, a cameraman for the US news agency APTN, was beaten by police after being summoned to Pristina police station. He was accused of filming in the Gornje Obrinje region where some 20 Albanian civilians had been shot and killed the previous week. (RSF)

SIERRA LEONE

Five journalists were sentenced to death for treason on 25 August after they were convicted of collaborating with the junta that ousted president Ahmed Tejan Kabbah in May 1997 (*Index* 4/1998). **Hilton Fyle**, managing director of WBIG (FM103) and a former BBC Africa Service presenter, **Ibrahim Kargbo**, managing editor of the weekly independent newspaper *Citizen*, **Gipu Felix George**, director of Sierra Leone Broadcasting Services, **Dennis Smith**, on-air broadcaster and **Olivia Mensah**, a newscaster, were among 59 civilians tried for treason following the restoration of President Kabbah in February. (A19)

On 15 September the Sierra Leone Association of Journalists released a statement requesting 'restraint' from foreigners demanding clemency for the five journalists sentenced to death for treason on 25 August. (CPJ)

SLOVAKIA

On 7 August **Vladimir Bacisin**, an investigative reporter for *Narodna Obroda*, was stopped by police for crossing the street on a red light, beaten and jailed. He was released the next day. Bacisin has recently published articles revealing illegal practices by firms linked with the ruling coalition. (RFE/RL)

On 8 September the Czech daily *Pravo* reported that **Pavel Rusko**, director of TV Markiza, was leaving the country after a warrant for his arrest was issued for alleged tax fraud, although this was denied by authorities. Rusko's concerns emanate from the station's take-over in August by close associates of the Counter-Intelligence Service head Ivan Lexa and Interior Minister Gustav Krajci. Rusko had previously refused the opportunity to buy the station himself as 'it would have meant serving the Meciar government'. (RFE/RL)

SOUTH AFRICA

Max Hamata, who wrote an article published in the *Mail and Guardian* titled

'Sex for Sale on Campus', has received threatening telephone calls according to a report on 22 September. Hamata's article related to prostitution at Peninsula Technikon, or 'Pentech'. He alleged that sex services were available from certain female students to both on and off-campus men. Hamata, a student of journalism, was called into the

office of the deputy-vice chancellor where he was questioned and accused of being 'disloyal' to the institution. (FXI)

Nine Cape Town policemen have been suspended from duty following the June assault on *Cape Argus* journalist **Thabo Mabaso** (*Index* 5/1998). West Metropolitan police chief said that the despite several requests, the police refused to attend an identification parade, which amounted to a failure to cooperate with the Internal Complaints Directorate and resulted in further delay in the criminal investigation. (FXI)

SRI LANKA

On 2 August President Chandrika Kumartunga said that the recently imposed censorship of war reporting (*Index* 4/1998) was 'likely to continue for some time' and that 'the local media will have to prove to us [the government] that they have learnt to be responsible' before restrictions are lifted. On 17 August the government further tightened censorship by banning the media from informing the public about the transfer of senior military officials. (RSF, Reuters)

Reuters stringer **Ponniah Manickavasagam** was released from custody without charge on 10 August (*Index* 5/1998). Two days later, his colleague, **Santhalingam Srigajan**, sought leave from the Supreme Court to file a fundamental rights application seeking his own immediate release and compensation. Both journalists, who work for the Tamil daily *Virakesari*, were arrested for alleged links with the Liberation Tigers of Tamil Eelam. (Reuters, *Midweek Mirror*)

Film producer **Gamini Fonseka** said on 13 August that the Ministry of Defence had stopped the production of his film *The Judgement*, which depicts the island cut in two along ethnic lines in 2005. Production ended after the ministry read the script, found it politically volatile and subsequently denied Fonseka the use of military equipment for filming. (Reuters, BBC World Service)

On 14 August officers of the Criminal Investigations Department (CID) entered the offices of two English-language weeklies, the *Sunday Times* and *Sunday Leader*, intimidated their staff and demanded to know from the editors the source of stories related to two government ministers. (Free Media Movement)

Somaratne Rajapakse, one of five members of the security forces sentenced to death in July for killing Tamils, was beaten by warders at Welikada prison on 23 August. Rajapakse was subsequently visited in hospital and threatened with death if he talked about the incident. The attack on Rajapakse apparently resulted from his refusal to sign a statement that he had been emotionally disturbed at the time he told the High Court that he could reveal where hundreds of murdered Tamils had been buried in the Jaffna Peninsula since 1996 (*Index* 5/1998). (AI, Asian Human

Rights Commission, Inform)

Thadshanamurthy Mathusoothanan, columnist for the Tamil-language *Saranihar* newspaper and editor of the Tamil-language bulletin of the Vibhavi Centre for Alternative Culture, was arrested by police on 26 August. Mathusoothanan has still not been released or charged. (Free Media Movement, Human Rights Action Committee-Sri Lanka, RSF)

Recent Publications: *Demanding Sacrifice: War and Negotiation in Sri Lanka* (Conciliation Resources, August 1998, 100 pp); *Judicial Independence in Sri Lanka* (Centre for the Independence of Jurists, September 1998, 186 pp).

SUDAN

The Arab Organisation for Human Rights asked the UN Security Council on 26 August to condemn the US bombing of a pharmaceutical plant in Khartoum and to send a fact-finding mission to investigate allegations that it had been producing chemical weapons. (*Arabic News*)

SWEDEN

In early October the Pope called off a meeting between himself and the Lutheran Archbishop of Sweden over Lutheran stance on homosexuality. Officially the meeting was postponed because of an exhibition of photographs in Uppsala Cathedral. The photographs by **Elisabeth Olsson** depict episodes from Christ's life, including a

transvestite Last Supper and Christ in various poses surrounded by homosexuals. Unofficially it is believed that the Pope objects to the Archbishop's support for the ordination of gay priests. (*Guardian*)

SWITZERLAND

On 12 August Credit Suisse and UBS the two largest Swiss banks finally agreed terms on a compensation deal with Jewish Holocaust groups over monies left in Swiss banks by victims of the Holocaust. Under the terms of the deal the banks will pay US$1.25 billion to survivors over a three-year period. The deal follows years of intense pressure from the Israeli and US governments. (*Financial Times*, *Guardian*)

On 25 August police raided the International Seminar on Globalisation and Resistance in Colgny, Geneva. The seminar was organised to explore ways of dealing with the social effects of the increasing global hegemony of transnational corporations. All participants, including journalists and human rights workers from 17 countries, were detained without charge for up to five hours. Many of the notebooks, videos and diaries confiscated by the police have yet to be returned to their owners. (TLIO)

TAJIKISTAN

Law enforcement officials on 19 August took three Pakistanis into custody on charges of distributing 'extremist' literature at mosques in Tajikistan. The three were apprehended in a Dushanbe mosque and were reported to be in possession of 'numerous' pieces of literature based on ideas espoused by Afghanistan's Taliban movement. (ITAR-TASS)

THAILAND

The organisers of the first Bangkok Film Festival were told by the censorship board on 27 September to suppress certain scenes from the New Zealand film *Topless Women Talk About Their Lives.* Scenes were blacked out by staff putting their hands in front of the projector. Two other entries were banned outright: *Bugis Street*, a Singaporean film about transvestites, and an unnamed Thai film deemed to be 'religiously provocative' (*Independent, Far East Economic Review*)

TOGO

On 6 August two editors' privately owned weeklies, **Augustin Asionbo** of *Tingo Tingo* and **Pamphile Gnimassou** of *Abito*, as well as **Elias Hounkali**, a journalist with the independent weekly *Nouveau Combat*, were arrested and placed in detention for 'attacking the honour' of the presidential couple. The arrests follow the publication in *Nouveau Combat* on 6 and 13 August of two articles entitled 'The Widow Mrs Bobi Mobutu demands from Mrs Badabnai Eyadéma her 17 Trunks of Jewellery Missing in Lomé' and 'Eyadéma Fishes for a Letter of Congratulations from Chirac'. The two editors-in-chief were reportedly arrested for

'complicity' in the publication of the articles, but Asionbo was exonerated and freed on 8 August. (RSF)

TURKEY

Sanar Yurdatapan, who was acquitted on 11 August in the trial of the pamphlet *'Freedom of Expression 2'*, is appealing against the decision (*Index* 3/1997, 3/1998, 5/1998). The pamphlet was published by 26 people from various professions who, by going to the State Security Court, denounced themselves before the public prosecutor. Charges were filed only against Yurdatapan, who is appealing on the principle of 'equality before the law'. (Med-TV)

On 19 August Radyo Ozgur, an Istanbul-based independent station, was suspended for a period of 90 days after broadcasting a programme *Tersname*, in which extracts were read out from an article in the daily *Gunluk Emek* which alleged that Kurdish villagers had been murdered by the police intelligence service, JITEM. (RSF)

On 19 August the private TV station ATV and the newspaper *Sabah* were attacked when shots were fired from a car at the Istanbul offices. Nobody was injured. (RSF)

Five teenage girls, aged between 11-15 years, were arrested and detained in September after dancing in the streets to raise money for a local orphanage. Police later said they believed the teenagers, who called themselves the 'Crazy Girls'

after their idols the Spice Girls, belonged to a Kurdish separatist group because the cardboard sign they had made to advertise the charity was coloured red, yellow and green – the Kurdish national colours. After being urged to confess to 'membership of an illegal organisation', the girls were released when their parents arrived at the police station with receipts from the orphanage as proof of their innocence. (Associated Press)

Ending a 17-year ban, an award-winning film about the ordeal of prisoners will finally be shown in cinemas in November, it was announced on 4 September. **Yilmaz Gunay**'s film *Yol* was co-winner of the Cannes Film Festival's 1982 Golden Palm award, but has never been released in Turkey. Gunay started directing the film while serving a 19-year sentence and completed it on his escape from prison in 1981. He died in exile in 1984. (Associated Press)

An NCO of Kurdish origin, **Kasim Cakun**, was dismissed on 14 September for openly supporting a peaceful solution to the Kurdish conflict. In June, the military leadership decided to dismiss 160 men for alleged Islamist activities. (Reuters)

Writer and journalist **Haluk Gerger** was released on 16 September after serving seven months in an Ankara prison. He had been charged for an article in a pro-Kurdish newspaper (*Index* 5/1998). (RSF)

On 19 September 22 human rights activists, including four

German women, were arrested at the 'Saturday Mothers' rally after police forcibly broke up the demonstration. The rallies are held by relatives of people who have 'disappeared' in police custody. (Agence France Presse)

A State Security court sentenced **Leyla Zana**, a Kurdish former deputy already serving a 15-year prison term, to another two years in jail for an article published by the pro-Kurdish People's Democracy Party (*Index* 1/1997). Sixteen others were also sentenced on a charge of 'inciting racial hatred'. Leyla Zana was awarded the European Parliament's Sakharov prize for freedom of expression in 1995. (Agence France Presse)

The Human Rights Foundation of Turkey has been awarded the European Human Rights Prize 1998 by the Committee of Ministers of the Council of Europe. The foundation's President, **Akin Birdal**, survived an attempt on his life earlier this year (*Index* 4/1998, 5/1998). (Human Rights Association)

Five journalists were attacked by a crowd of demonstrators at a 28 September protest against the imprisonment of former Islamist mayor Recep Tayip Erdogan. **Ahmet Dumanli** from the daily *Milliyet*, **Ali Oksuz**, cameraman for Star TV, **Serhat Sunay**, cameraman for TGRT TV, **Adnan Gul**, reporter for the daily *Yeni Yuzyil* and **Levent Ozturk**, reporter for Kanal D television, were threatened by the Islamists. (RSF)

Dogu Perincek, leader of the Worker's Party (IP), began a 14-month sentence on 28 September for a television election address in 1991, broadcast on the private TV channel TRT. Charges relating to links between the IP and the PKK (Kurdistan Worker's Party) were not upheld. (Med-TV, AKIN, *Cumhuriyet*)

Recep Tayyip Erdogan, Istanbul's mayor and popular Islamist political figure, was sentenced on 30 September to 10 months and banned from politics for life for reciting an extract from a poem at a political rally in the south-east last year (*Index* 3/1998). In a continuation of the crackdown on Islamism, **Bekir Yildiz**, mayor of Sincan, received a sentence of four years and seven months for calling for Islamic rule at a rally in 1997 (*Index* 2/1997). Both had been accused of inciting religious hatred. (Associated Press)

MED-TV, the Kurdish satellite channel, was again jammed by illegally transmitted signals on 9 and 10 October during the live transmission of the Turkish news (*Index* 2/1997, 5/1997). (Med-TV)

The weekly newspaper *Halk Icin Kurtulus* (*Index* 5/1997) was raided on 7 October and 24 people arrested including the owners, editors and staff. The State Security court also closed down the paper for one month. (Human Rights Action)

The country's first woman publisher, **Ayse Nur Zarakolu** was awarded the newly-created International Freedom to Publish Award on 7 October. Zarakolu, through her company Belge International, has been publishing books for over 20 years, many of which have been banned (*Index* 3/1997, 4/1997). (*Turkish Probe*)

On 12 October three journalists from the Islamist press in Istanbul were arrested. **Abdurrahman Dilipak**, editor of the daily *Akit*, **Ekrem Kiziltas**, editor-in-chief of the *Milli Gazete* daily and **Ahmet Tasgetiren**, editor of *Yeni Safak*, were accused of inciting racial hatred in articles they wrote on the demonstrations against the ban on headscarves in universities. (RSF)

TURKMENISTAN

The former presidential spokesperson **Durdumuhammed Gurbanov**, who has criticised the government in the international media this year, was arrested on 1 September in Ashgabat on charges of embezzlement, mismanagement of funds and misuse of state property. After a 7 September protest in Ashgabat by 30 people demanding Gurbanov's release, and an appeal by Amnesty International, he was released on 8 September. (RFE/RL)

Opposition leader **Durdymurat Khojamuhammedov** was abducted on 4 September, driven to the outskirts of Ashgabat and severely beaten. The attack drew protests from Human Rights Watch which wrote: 'In Turkmenistan, where public order is enforced with extreme vigilance, such an act of brutality could not be carried out without official sanction.' Khojamuhammedov, who leads the unregistered Democratic Development Party, had been incarcerated in a psychiatric hospital from February 1996 to April 1998, when he was let out on the eve of President Niyazov's visit to Washington (*Index* 4/1998). (RFE/RL)

UNITED KINGDOM

On 14 August the Association of Chief Officers of Probation called for curbs on the powers of newspapers to report the movements of paedophiles released from custody. They made their call following the rise in the number of vigilante groups preventing the resettlement of sex offenders. (*Independent*)

In early September the European Commission on Human Rights ruled that a convicted drug dealer, **Michael Govell**, had been denied redress from the police watchdog, the Police Complaints Authority (PCA). The Commission found that the complaints system was open to abuse as the minister responsible for the police, Jack Straw, also appoints, dismisses and, in some cases, guides the members of the PCA. Straw said that the Home Office would look into the viability of a new independent complaints body. (*Observer*)

On 3-4 September 1998, in the wake of the Omagh bombing, the government convened an emergency sitting of parliament to consider the Criminal Justice (Terrorism and Conspiracy) Bill.

The bill gives police unprecedented powers to jail suspects involved in domestic terrorism and foreign nationals planning, or accused of, terrorist acts. MPs and civil liberties groups expressed concerns that the bill was being rushed through parliament without detailed debate or scrutiny. Nonetheless, it was passed overwhelmingly in both houses. (*Guardian*)

On 19 September food-engineering conglomerate Monsanto was granted extensive injunctions at the High Court against members of **genetiX snowball**, including their press officer. Under the terms of the injunction, the six named injunctees must not trespass on the scores of farms currently hosting trials of Monsanto's modified crops or conspire with others to do so. (*Guardian*)

The European Court of Human Rights ruled on 23 September that police had violated the right to freedom of speech of three arms-trade protesters – **Andrea Needham, David Polden** and **Christopher Cole** – who were arrested after raising a banner which read 'Work for Peace not War' at an aeronautical conference in London. (*Guardian*)

On 24 September the Iranian government announced that it was disassociating itself from the *fatwa* imposed on **Salman Rushdie** after the publication of *The Satanic Verses* nine years earlier. Despite assurances of Rushdie's safety from Iranian foreign minister Kamal Kharrazi, however, hardline groups inside and outside Iran

insisted that the *fatwa* was an irrevocable edict. (*Guardian, International Herald Tribune, Times*)

On 30 September the Crown Prosecution Service decided not to prosecute the University of Central England on grounds of obscenity after police seized a book of Robert Mapplethorpe photographs. The book featured two photographs of gay men performing own acts and the university and the book's publisher Jonathan Cape were warned that they could face charges under the 1959 Obscene Publications Act. (*Guardian, Daily Telegraph*)

At the Blackpool party conference on 30 September, Home Secretary Jack Straw announced a review of the proposed freedom of information legislation that had been one of the centrepieces of the election manifesto. Straw, who is known to be hostile to the bill, took over responsibility for the legislation from David Clark who had promised to put forward a draft by the end of September. Labour backbencher Rhodri Morgan told a fringe meeting that the freedom of information issue would demonstrate whether New Labour was 'genuinely libertarian or whether it is run by control freaks and spin doctors' (*Guardian*)

It was reported on 2 October that **Suzi Clark**, former editor of the University of Middlesex's *North Circular* magazine, had lost her battle against 'redeployment' after her attempt to print an article critical of the campus's 'culture of fearful conformity' (*Index* 4/1998). Clark was reported to be moving to the university library.(*Times Higher Education Supplement*)

On 7 October Home Secretary Jack Straw announced the introduction of visas for all Slovaks, a decision that was seen to be a way of stemming the tide of Slovak Romanies into the country. (*Guardian, Financial Times*)

On 13 October an inquiry into the BSE crisis heard that officials at the Ministry of Agriculture, Fisheries & Food had resisted telling ministers and the public that BSE- infected offal had entered the human food chain. Sir Kenneth Calman, the former chief medical officer, had repeatedly issued assurances that British beef was safe, but he told the Inquiry that 'safe' did not necessarily mean that there was 'no possible risk'. (*Guardian*)

In London on 17 October police placed the ailing former Chilean dictator General Augusto Pinochet under restraint following the issuance of Interpol Red Notice, which alleges his involvement in the torture and murder of Spanish citizens between 1973 and 1983. He was expected to appear before magistrates after his recovery to face extradition to Spain, where two judges, Baltasar Garzon and Manuel Garcia Castellon, seek to question him. (*Observer*)

USA

An international dispute has broken out over who owns the rights to the yellow 'smiley-face' invented in 1973 by an American contract artist. Franklin Loufrani, a Parisian who has owned the French copyright for the symbol since 1971 and now owns the mark in more than 80 countries, has applied for the EU trademark which would give him exclusive rights. A Japanese company also is claiming the trademark, which it registered in Japan in 1989. (*The Times*)

The CIA gave the Dalai Lama over one million dollars a year for most of the 1960s for operations against China, according to State Department documents published in September. The money supported Tibetan guerillas in Nepal, a training base in Colorado, 'Tibet Houses' to publicise the Tibetan cause and university educations for Tibetan operatives. (*International Herald Tribune*)

In early September, Rupert Murdoch forced the Fox Network to give up plans for a film based on a book about the sexual harassment charges against his friend, Supreme Court Justice Clarence Thomas. The book upon which the film was to be based, *Strange Justice*, was nominated for a National Book Award in 1994 for its 'meticulous investigation.' (*International Herald Tribune*)

Dmitri Nabokov, son of Vladimir Nabokov, author of *Lolita*, filed a suit in US federal court on 8 October to prevent the publication of the English translation of *Lo's Diary*, a book written from Lolita's point of view in 1995 by Italian writer **Pia Pera**. The suit claims the book is a 'rip-off', but US publishers Farrar, Straus & Giroux say *Lo's Diary* falls within fair use standards set in American copyright law. (*Guardian*)

Recent publications: *USA: Rights For All*, (AI, 10/98).

UZBEKISTAN

Journalists **Vitaly Ponomarev** and **Nikolai Mitrokhin** of Moscow's Panorama Agency were beaten by five or six men in Tashkent on 1 August, shortly after their meeting with human rights activist Marat Zakhidov. The assault is believed to be connected to the journalists' collating of information about the repression of religious organisations. (Glasnost Defence Foundation)

On 3 August the Supreme Court confirmed the 11-year prison sentence handed down in June against Samarkand radio journalist **Shadi Mardiev** (*Index* 5/1998). His lawyer has appealed to the court's plenary session. (Glasnost Defence Foundation)

The Russian daily *Vremya MN* published on 1 September a list of potential trouble-makers that the government has reportedly distributed to leaders in villages and city districts. Leaders are formally instructed to follow up residents between 16 and 32 years of age who have left the city to find out what they are doing now. Other subjects for surveillance include traders travelling to Saudi Arabia, Turkey, Pakistan, or Iran; those who call upon women to adhere to Islamic codes of conduct; anyone who has links with Wahabbis; anyone who has ever grown a beard; any man who has more than one wife; any family members of known Wahabbis who have reached 18 years of age and are not serving in the armed forces; and any girls who were married off before they turned 16. (RFE/RL)

VIETNAM

Doan Viet Hoat, the founder of the pro-democracy *Freedom Forum* newsletter who was sentenced to 20 years' imprisonment in March 1993, was released on 2 September and immediately flown to Bangkok. On arrival, he expressed a longing to return to his homeland. (Associated Press)

Poet and writer **Nguyen Van Thuan** was released in an amnesty in early September, it was reported on 9 September. (PEN)

YEMEN

On 22 July poet **Ahmed Nasser Gaber**, member of the Executive Committee of the Arab Writers' Union, was arrested upon the orders of the Political Security and Central Security forces of Zingibar along with 10 members of the **League of the Sons of Yemen (RAY) Party** for organising a peaceful mass demonstration. The demo, due to take place on 23 July, was banned.

On 8 August **Awadh Kasheem**, correspondent with the daily *Attariq* in Dawaan, eastern Yemen, was arrested without a warrant and accused of 'incitement to violence'. Kashmeem was involved in investigating fraud in telecommunications and was released after 30 hours of detention. (RSF)

It was reported on 11 August that 'firewalls' have been placed against internet sites deemed offensive by authorities in preparation for local access to the internet to commence by the end of the year. (Reuters).

Ali Dahmess, Jaar correspondant for the weekly *Athouri*, was arrested by security forces and sent to the Criminal Investigation Department, according to a report on 27 August. The director of the department is known to be related to one of the two tribes involved in a property dispute Dahmess had reported upon days prior to his arrest. (RSF 27 August)

It was reported on 10 September that **Mohammed Sadek Al-Odaini**, a reporter for daily *Al Mithaq*, has been detained without charge since December 1997. He has since been been accused of murdering a passer-by while being assaulted by unidentified men. Al-Odaini swears his innocence. (RSF)

ZAMBIA

The Lusaka High Court on 21 October found the independent daily *Post* guilty of contempt for commenting on the court's delay in incriminating two politicians suspected of involvement in the failed coup in October 1997. Justice Japhet Banda was making a ruling on an application by the attorney general over the *Post*'s 19 October edition which declared that the two politicians, Nakatindi Wina and Dean Mung'omba, were innocent. Wina is the ruling MMD women's chairperson while Mung'omba is president. of the opposition Zambia Democratic Congress (ZDC). (*Times of Zambia*)

Compiled by: Suzanne Fisher, Regina Jere-Malanda, Daniel Rogers (Africa); Andrew Kendle, Melissa Ong, Meera Selvananthan (Asia); Rupert Clayton, Simon Martin (eastern Europe and CIS); Dolores Cortés (south and central America); Arif Azad, Gill Newsham, Randip Panesar (Middle East), Andrew Elkin (north America and Pacific); Tony Callaghan (UK and western Europe).

CEGERXWIN

Kurdistan

Kurdistan, my Kurdistan;
Humbled; by others possessed;
Garden of my roses, Kurdistan;
Of our grieving, the painful cause.

In your loftiness my Kurdistan
Nestle hamlets, towns embraced by you;
And to die is the reward
for worshippers of this land of mine.

Rivers crossing meadows, spilling
Onto fields like painted silver lines
between hilly vineyards
And endowing with beauty my Kurdistan.

Paupers are we, walking on your soil,
Pitilessly plundered by foes
Of nature's richness and bounty,
Haunted by seemingly endless poverty.

Your luckless people robbed
Of many-splendoured golds
while the tower-shrines of Kohrash and Ardashir
Are defiled by ever-watching stranger's probing eyes.

O, mother of the Tigris and Euphrates!
Shameless with no honour is the Kurd who betrays you;
My heart bleeding with other Kurdish hearts,
Yet still alive for you my Kurdistan.

Lyrics: Cegerxwin Vocal: Shivan Perwer
Translation: Chahin Baker
See disc notes p8/9

JUDITH VIDAL-HALL

A gig too far

Oran, goes the saying, gave Algeria raï, Kabylia, home to the
Berbers, their songs, both of them symbols of the widely felt
resistance to the machinations of the military-political clans in
government and to growing fundamentalist violence. The Berber
singers, of whom Lounès Matoub, assassinated in June 1998 at a fake
road-block just outside Tizi-Ouzou, 110kms from Algiers, was the most
provocative, also articulated the rage of their people in the face of the
regime's renewed determination to impose Arabic as the sole official
language throughout Algeria.

Lounès Matoub had been one of the great voices of the Kabylie,
radical, outspoken and often controversial. His last song – and one that
many thought had led directly to his death – was a double challenge to
the regime. Not only did it denounce the government's alliance with the
Islamists, it openly mocked one of its sacred cows by setting the
inflammatory words to the tune of Algeria's national anthem.

Matoub's death unleashed the pent-up hostility to government that
had been more or less contained since the introduction of multi-party
politics in 1989 As news leaked out, even before the official
announcement on state TV and radio, crowds poured onto the streets of
Tizi-Ouzou (seat of local government in Kabylie) shouting anti-
government slogans, threatening to set fire to government buildings and
defacing signs in Arabic that had replaced those in Berber. 'Pouvoir
assassin! We want to live long enough to bring down this corrupt regime
that has killed Lounès and is in the process of excluding us from our own
country!' Lines to phone-in radio programmes were jammed with
outpourings of grief, anger and frustration.

Born in 1956 in Taourit-Mousa, near Tizi-Ouzou, Matoub made his
first album, '*Ay Izem*' (The lion) in 1978. It was an instant hit and was
quickly followed by a second, '*Ayemma a'zizen*' (Dear Mother). When

anti-government demonstrations swept through Tizi-Ouzou in April 1980, his songs were the anthems of the protesters. Along with an older generation of singers that included people like Lounis Aït Menguellet, Ferhat M'henni, and Idir, whose music had been at the forefront of Berber cultural resistance to forced arabisation since the early 1970s, all his songs were banned. It did not prevent his impassioned defence of the Berber language nor his attacks on the fundamentalists, those 'grim reapers of the stars' as he called them in 'Kenza', a song dedicated to the daughter of the writer and journalist Tahar Djaout, murdered by Islamists in Algiers in June 1993 (*Index* 4&5/1994).

Matoub favoured rock over the more lyrical style of Menguellet or Idir; poetry was frequently sacrificed to militant sentiments: 'Companion of the revolution/Though your body rots/Your name lives for ever' he sang in 'The revolutionary' on the album 'My mother's lament'. His radical stance won him a large following among the younger generation, but alienated others in the Berber community who saw him as too confrontational for anyone's good. On 25 September 1994, at the height of the attacks on Algerian writers, journalists and intellectuals critical of the Islamists, he was kidnapped and held for a fortnight, allegedly by the GIA.

He was not alone in rousing the ire of government and Islamists. Singers had been a particular target of the fanatical and puritanical Islamic extremists for whom music, song and dance were among the prime evils of a society it sought to restore to the mythical 'purity' of true Islam. On 24 September 1994, the young raï singer Cheb Hasni was killed by the GIA; raï 'king' Cheb Khaled left for exile under threat of death for 'infringing social taboos' and 'stirring [Algeria's] youth to rebellion'; Cheb Aziz, Lila Amara and the producer Rachid were all victims of the violence engulfing Algeria.

Matoub was among the lucky ones. He was returned by his captors a fortnight later, intact but with stories of a trial and mock execution, spared only when he swore under pain of death not to sing again. A few months later, he was playing to packed halls in Paris, where he remained for much of 1995.

By 1996 he was back, provocative as ever and at the receiving end of criticism even from within his own community, many of whom remained sceptical of his kidnapping, accusing him of having made a pact with the devil out of fear for his life. He had refused to condemn the shooting of Cheb Hasni only a day before his own disappearance; colleagues scented a taste for martyrdom in his increasingly confrontational music, fearing it might incite his political associates to mount some sort of 'coup'. They sensed a taste for martyrdom and kept their distance.

By June 1998 it was all over: Matoub was dead. Just one more statistic in the vast toll of Algeria's civil war, but for the Kabylie a loss that has yet to be replaced. ❑

JVH

Open letter to the Powers That Be

'The truth! Shout it out
Send the lies packing
Only those who have lived through it know what is shaking this
country...
Look further, please! We know who's killing!
The government, a heavy burden to bear
But it seems nothing stirs them
They know tomorrow offers no respite
They've created a monster that's bogging them down
Oh! Oh! Oh! Oh! Oh! How can you love a girl you can't see?

How can you find out what the veil hides? Mmmmmh!
(*Ironically*)
Never believe them, they're the enemies of life
Do you remember, can you recall
Bouyali[1], and the people he went with?
No need to look further, it's Nahnah,[2]
The gateway to death and oppression, with whom he'd
signed up
In a pact of aggression against the people
And yes! Today we can see them!
There up in power. They've had a change of heart ...
They snuck into power on the tips of their toes and time
means nothing to them ...
How long did they wait for Khalida[3]
She who troubled their sleep? Ah
Yeh! Yeh! Yeh! Yeh!
Don't dare imagine what they would have done if they'd
caught her ...
Useless to wait on hope, to believe in the virtues of patience,
we men of the mountains will never have power, no matter how
cultured, how far we pull ourselves up ...
They've repainted our country in the colours of religion and
Arabic.
Treachery! Treachery! Treachery!
If you think they'll ever relinquish the keys to the Gateway,
Forget it, you're far too naive...
With our roots and our clearness of vision we will rid Algeria of
its
Treachery! Treachery! Treachery! ...

*From 'Open letter to the powers that be' from Lounès Matoub's album
'Algeriassic Park' (Blue Silver/Virgin). Translated from Kabyle by* **Rabah
Mezouane** *and from French by* **JVH**

1 Mustapha Bouyali headed the first armed Islamic group in 1986
2 Sheik Nahnah, leader of the main legal Islamist party, in a power-sharing arrangement with the regime
3 Khalida Messaoudi, leading Algerian feminist and member of the *Rassemblement pour la culture et la démocratie*, one of the two main
Berber parties

NOAM BEN-ZEEV

The Deluge and the Ring

If the directors of Israel's two major radio stations – *Kol Israel* (The Voice of Israel, owned by the Israeli Broadcasting Authority) and the army radio *Galey Zahal* (IDF Waves, managed by the Israeli Defense Forces) – are to be believed, there is no such thing as music censorship in Israel. Nothing is banned, only 'treated with special care' – or simply not played on air. Songs with explicit sexually or violently abusive language, songs like 'After Us the Deluge', written in the midst of a war and offensive to the parents of fallen soldiers, Si Helman's 'Shooting and crying', one of a number of protest song written during the Palestinian Uprising [Intifada] in the 80s – and no longer banned – are among the special cases that attracted the less than enthusiastic attention of those who make up the stations' play list. Even today, the Israeli songs of the Intifada are seldom heard; Palestinian, or Arab Israeli music is just one more victim of the wholesale discrimination Palestinian Israelis suffer in Israel.

While the picture is less rosy than those in authority would have us believe, things are a good deal better than in the 1960s when the cultural and economic gap between Sephardi Jews who had immigrated from the Arab world and the politically dominant Ashkenazi Jews from western Europe, translated into a generalised discrimination against the newborn Israeli Rock'n'Roll of the former.

The 1960s and 70s also saw some genuine, straightforward censorship: the Beatles were barred from visiting Israel; songs by 'The High Windows' were banned on religious grounds; a Hebrew version of a George Brassens' number, 'The Will', was banned for one line – 'After I die find yourself a husband who will use my boots and my bed'; and 'The Battle Hill', that made it to the top of the pops in its first week, was immediately taken out of the list and effectively silenced for ever. It sang of a real battle in the Six Day War, a battle that took a high toll of lives and, notwithstanding the song's enormous popularity, was not broadcast.

The worst victim of this period, however, was neither pop star nor Sephardi rocker. When Israel's foremost playwright, Hanoch Levin, then still very young, wrote his *Queen of the Bath,* a sharp and audacious attack on the folly of war and the futile adoration of heroism and death, the play was literally torn down by an angry (and well-organized) crowd. Its witty, and at times hair-raising songs, are not heard even today on the radio. To all intents and purposes they were 'disappeared'.

But the big music story in Israel when it comes to banning is about classical music. Until a few years ago, Bach's Passions led the classical hit list. Fearing the wrath of an audience that would find their texts anti-semitic because they blame the Jews for the death of Christ, the Israeli Philharmonic Orchestra simply excluded these masterpieces of western music from its repertoire.

Nazi collaborators like conductors Herbert von Karajan and Karl Boehm, the singer Elizabeth Schwarzkopf and composers like Rikhard Strauss and Karl Orff have always aroused the opposition of a population that still lives the horrors of the Holocaust. Yet only Strauss ever suffered a complete boycott by orchestras and the radio, and even this was broken at the beginning of the 1990s by Noam Sheriff, conductor of the Rishon LeZion Orchestra, in response to the growing public demand to hear the works they were being denied.

And then there is Richard Wagner. The ban on all his works has been put to the test many times in the last 50 years but remains as unshakeable as ever. Wagner was a self declared anti-semite and, although dead long before Hitler came to power, in Israel, the man and his music are totally identified with Nazism. As long as there are Holocaust survivors who will be deeply wounded and offended by the performance of his work, Wagner issue will not go away and his music will not be performed publicly.

Nor do Israeli modern classicists fare much better. Three years ago, 'Upon Thy Ruins, Ofrah' by Arie (Arik) Shapira was aired on Israel's classical music station The Voice of Music. (Ofrah is an extreme-right Jewish settlement in Occupied Palestine.) The station was swamped with outraged protests and the director meekly apologised. Shapira, winner of the Israel Prize and an uncompromising left-wing critic of the government and establishment, is a radical composer who makes no attempt to caress the ears of his listeners. Though widely acknowledged throughout Europe, he is rarely performed in Israel where his radical views on politics and music are no more popular than his compositions.

Other Israeli composers suffer the same fate. 'There were red lists which we all knew, mostly the music of Nazi collaborators and, for a while, music manufactured by companies that gave in to the Arab Boycott on Israel, like Phillips,' recalls composer Oded Zehavi of the time he worked for the radio. 'But there were also black lists, known only to the directors knew, not the humble editors.

'Kol Israel ruled that it would not broadcast original music unless it had been recorded by the station itself. Censorship worked even at that preliminary stage: if you didn't record controversial works in the first place, you had no problems with what or what not to ban. If you didn't belong to the establishment you had no chance of being recorded and were silenced. If you looked at the composers who were 'in' you wouldn't find minorities – Arabs, women, Sephardi Jews – among them. Until 15 or 20 years ago, you had to be part of the scene, belong to the Academy of Music, in which the same establishment composers were teaching. If there were radical composers at that time we shall probably never know.' ❑

Noam Ben-Zeev *is the music critic for the Israeli daily* Haaretz

UMIT OZTURK

Singing of home

ÜMIT ÖZTÜRK *Tell us about yourself, your family and background, how you became a singer and why you and your songs were banned in Turkey?*

SHIVAN PERWER I was born in Urfa [In South East Anatolia or Turkish Kurdistan]. My whole family were music lovers; I still remember my father singing Kurdish folk songs all the time. When I was a teenager, I started to visit the cities and met Kurdish people from Iranian, Iraqi and Syrian Kurdistan who were studying in Turkey. Those people had a great influence on me, prompting me to go deeper and wider into the music.

Soon after, in late-1972, I made my first public appearance. I still remember the first Kurdish song I sang: it was '*Welate me Kurdistan'e*' (My Homeland is Kurdistan). But when you raise the matter of Kurdish identity, even in music, you invite trouble. I had stirred up the hornet's nest and the trouble started.

Do you mean your songs were banned because they were in Kurdish, or because they said things the Turkish government didn't like?

Both. Not only did my songs spread the Kurdish voice in Kurdish, a language that is banned, its existence officially denied, the message of my songs became more and more politicised over the years. In 1974, when I started my musical outcry publicly, I didn't know a great deal about the history, politics and social agony of Kurdistan; I was just an enthusiastic, good Kurdish lad, that's all. Never mind the variety of music, I had no knowledge, let alone skills, of the music of my nation in a deeper sense.

However, over the years, I realised that many singers - although they were all Kurdish in origin - were singing either Turkish songs or Kurdish songs translated into Turkish. I felt someone should have the audacity to fight against the ban on singing in Kurdish. It was ludicrous that Kurds could only listen to Kurdish music on radio programmes from Yerevan, Baghdad and elsewhere; never in their own country.

I decided to fight the taboo and went for it head on. This made the Turkish regime exceedingly uncomfortable and was followed by an instant ban on my music. In the eyes of the Turkish regime, the language and the content of my songs together formed a kind of 'double trouble'. I came to Europe in 1976 and have lived in exile ever since with my wife Gulistan and my son Serxwebun. I've produced two dozen solo albums, four more with my wife Gulistan, two albums of songs for children and four video albums.

Are all your songs 'political' in that they reflect your thoughts and emotions about your country, about what is happening to your people? Or, are they simply lyrical expressions of your private feelings?

As I said, when I decided to fight the ban on Kurdish identity through music, I was already aware that it was also a must to sing revolutionary songs on the daily life, agony and poverty of Kurdish people. But I was always careful not to perform in a 'monotone'. That is to say, it's so very easy to fall into the trap of becoming nothing more than a singer of agitprop. But I wanted constantly to broaden my repertoire, add to its diversity? In the early years, I didn't have enough material: all I had to work on were the poems of a few Kurdish poets. However, if you're stubborn you just keep on looking and you find. Before too long, you're creating your own lyrics and composing your own songs. That's what I did. I've always tried to offer my people songs to suit a wide range of tastes: from myths and legends to desperate love stories; from anonymous folk songs to revolutionary songs of defiance and resistance. I've also tried to help Kurdish music in general develop in new directions. For instance, one of my favourite songs, '*Kine Em*' (Who am I?) is an attempt to incorporate rock into the more traditional Kurdish style. Looking back, I can see it worked quite well. Of course, some of my songs interpret my emotions as a Kurd, as a musician, as an exile.

Music and song have apparently been an integral part of Kurdish culture. From weddings to funerals, Kurds have a song for every moment in life. Is it true that your songs were once used as an anaesthesia in Iraqi Kurdistan?

Yes, I was told about this. One of the Iraqi *Peshmergas* had been wounded fighting in the mountains and was taken to have the bullets removed. Because the medical facilities were inadequate, they made him listen to my songs so that he wouldn't feel the pain. I think the reason some of my songs are seen as 'painkillers' is because I myself have felt the pain, suffering, grief and agony of my people as an individual. If you have experienced something in your own life, then you feel it all the time and can interpret it in your songs.

You are known as the leading Kurdish singer of today. Who were the great Kurdish singers and musicians of the past? Did any of them have problems with the governments of the day?

There were a number of great Kurdish singers whom I call my 'seeds of inspiration': Meryam Xan, Kabus Axa, Isa Berwari, Hesen Cizrawi, Hesen Axaye and Arif Cizrawi, for instance. Of course they had trouble with the authorities and faced persecution by various regimes. But they never compromised, never unfurled the white flag of surrender. For instance, Arif Cizrawi was once asked what his intentions were in singing in Kurdish: did he have a hidden agenda or was he simply greedy for a career? He is said to have answered: 'I want the entire world to understand Kurdish, so that it can listen to me and understand our message.'

Can you still write songs and sing in exile?

I have been writing and singing in the same spirit since the very first day of exile. Although I still compose songs based on Kurdish folklore and poems, every new album includes some of my own lyrics.

How do you use your music in exile? Who do you play for and where?

I tour the world giving concerts and this occupies most of my time, but I also work on my new albums. I usually sing in gigs organised by Kurdish and Turkish community organisations and groups in exile, especially during *Newroz* [Kurdish New Year's Day, 21 March] celebrations. I also take part in multicultural solidarity gigs and this gives me the opportunity to get Kurdish culture across to other communities.

Has your music changed in exile?

The conditions and opportunities in Europe have improved and enriched my musical style. For instance, there is no fear of the police at our door, waiting to raid the concert or arrest us. This peace of mind helps the music blossom freely. However, it is not simply the civil liberties we enjoy in Europe, but also a variety of encouragement and support. For example, in some European countries, the technical and financial support for minorities provided by the authorities helps them preserve and revitalise their cultural identity. Given all these freedoms and benefits, you can concentrate and push your art forward in new, more colourful paths.

What is the pain of exile for a musician? Would you go home if you could?

If you don't keep the faith, you are a dead man walking. Exile is a burden but you can't let this heaviness wear you down. The worst thing is the deprivation of so many things that make up home; the inevitable sense that something is always missing from the picture. But you can survive, revive even. I feel my entire body is here, minus my heart. And my heart still lies in my homeland. Whenever this missing piece is placed in the incomplete picture, then we can talk about an absolute happiness. So, yes, there is no question I would go back my homeland if I could; but this is out of the question.

Can people in Kurdistan/Turkey listen to your music? Is the music banned as well as the musician?

My music has been available for listeners in Turkey for the past few years. However, there is always a *de facto* ban or restriction. Record companies have been able to reproduce my tapes and CDs, but people who buy them can always be harassed or detained arbitrarily by the authorities. People in other parts of Kurdistan have better access to my music than Kurds in Turkey. As for myself, the musician, I am totally banned in Turkey. ❑

Ümit Öztürk *is a journalist from Turkey living in London. He is the vice-chair of Amnesty International's journalists' network*

KAVEH BASMENJI

Songs of divine love

Iranians are increasingly tuning in to the new wave of 'revolutionary' pop that combines state-of-the-art production techniques and western melodies with traditional Iranian elements and lyrics about divine love

In the music shops on Tehran's bustling Revolution Avenue, young Iranians eagerly ask when the latest album by Khashaiar Etemadi will be available. 'Sorry, sold out,' says Reza, a record store clerk.

Etemadi is one of a dozen singers who has jumped to popularity in the past year on the tide of the new pop music. Some critics say his appeal is strong because he sounds like Dariush, an Iranian exile in Los Angeles whose records are smuggled into the country and snatched up by eager listeners. Etemadi dismisses the charge. His most popular song drew much criticism because its lyrics were written by Ahmad Shamloo, a veteran poet who is frequently denounced by suspicious conservatives as a 'wayward westernised lackey' and much of whose work is banned in Iran.

In Vali-Asr Street, one of Tehran's main thoroughfares, young men standing on the pavement whisper to passers-by, 'I have new tapes, I have new films,' mainly contraband music from an Iranian expatriate community in Los Angeles that is so big and influential it is known here as 'Irangeles'. But more and more people are turning to locally-produced, officially-approved pop music. 'The music is nice, the vocals are powerful, and the lyrics aren't important, because you tend to forget them,' says Shahrokh, a 21-year-old university student.

Revolutionary pop songs are mostly created by mounting lyrics about divine love and admiration for nature onto an off-beat, slow melody.

Part of its appeal is undoubtedly the similarities in vocal style to that of expatriate Iranian artists, officially banned inside Iran but widely available.

For nearly 15 years after the 1979 Islamic revolution, the only legal music in Iran was war hymns, traditional songs or anodyne instrumentals. Persian-language pop music, mostly contraband from Los Angeles, was smuggled across the Gulf from Dubai.

During the first years of the revolution, there was pressure from the traditionalist clergy to put a total ban on music, which was turned down by Ayatollah Ruhollah Khomeini. In one of his most famous rulings, Khomeini said that if a piece of music was not 'intoxicating', there was nothing wrong with it.

In today's more relaxed Iran, fostered in part by the social and political reforms of President Mohammad Khatami, tolerance towards western-style music is growing. Surprisingly, given that radio and television are controlled by the conservative faction which frequently expresses concern over the dilution of revolutionary and Islamic principles and fears of a foreign cultural invasion, state-run television even shows a video clip on the evils of drug addiction with instrumental music by British rocker Eric Clapton.

However, pop music from the West, in particular from 'Irangeles' still dominates most private parties, including raucous weddings. Revolutionary pop does not offer the necessary beat for dancing. But for many young people, the Los Angeles music is losing its magic, because it has grown increasingly out of touch with contemporary Iranian society. 'It's becoming boring. I don't listen to it any more except at parties,' said 23-year-old Afsaneh. ❏

Kaveh Basmenji is Reuters' correspondent in Iran

HENGAMEH AKHAVAN

Silent Spring

As usual in Iran, it's the women who are at the sharp end of musical censorship

Mehdi Es'heqi-Abarqu'i *We read in the papers that* Bahar's *(Spring) concert was postponed for a week. What was the problem?*

Hengameh Akhavan Back in the winter of 1476 [1998], the *Shahr-e Rey* Welfare Department decided to arrange a special women's concert and to use the money raised from the performance for the homeless children in its care. But since a women's music group is always faced with difficulties, our problem in the first instance was to get a permit. After innumerable letters to various departments and the dogged persistence of myself and one of the employees of *Shahr-e Rey*, we finally crossed every possible hurdle and barrier and got a permit for the concert. But, after getting the permit, an official at *Ershad* [Islamic culture and guidance ministry] said: 'You cannot publicise the concert in the press. You cannot... you cannot...'

Finally, we navigated our way through all the difficulties and the day of the performance arrived. The members of the group and the audience were gathered in the cultural centre for the performance when, a few moments before the performance, they told us there was a technical (sound) problem and that the concert had to be postponed. At that point, I really didn't know what to say to the members of the group who were very upset, or to all the music lovers who had come to the centre with such enthusiasm.

However, I'm happy to say that with the co-operation of the people in charge of the cultural centre, *Ershad* and so on, the problem was solved and we were able to perform the programme a few days later.

Did you ask the officials what the problem had been?

The question I want to ask the officials is, 'If you are in favour of women's concerts why do you then say don't publicise the concert in the press? If you really don't want the performance to take place, don't issue a permit. That way we'll all know where we stand. If, on the other hand, you do approve of them and issue permits, then what's the meaning of all this?'

They are inconsistent in the way they treat women artists. For example, the ... group, which is much less experienced, has been less active and possibly even has a poorer programme, manages to get permits without any problem. However, when it comes to issuing a permit for the *Bahar* group, which consists of much more experienced performers, they try our patience to the limit with their bureaucracy and red tape.

The other problem is that we're not allowed to make audio or video recordings during the performance. Most important of all, when we had our recent four-night performance at the Bahman cultural centre [in Tehran], at the end of the programme they said that the concert time had been agreed for 7.00pm–9.00pm and we had to leave the hall immediately. The audience was asking us to perform *Morgh-e Sahar* [Dawn Bird], but the officials wouldn't allow it. They said since we hadn't given them a copy of the lyrics beforehand, we couldn't perform it. This, too, upset me and the other members of the group, as well as the audience...

Tell us about your own life. When did you turn to music and singing?

I was born in 1334 [1955–56] in Fuman and I lived there until I finished primary school. My mother was a housewife and my father worked for the transport department in Gilan Province [near the Caspian Sea]. I'm the youngest in the family. Everyone in our family has good voices. My late father had a very good voice. My mother's voice is incredibly strong, warm, melodious and gentle. You'll rarely find all these qualities in one person's voice. My mother is not familiar with the formal modes of [Iranian] music and her lovely voice is just a God-given gift. My brother has a beautiful, strong voice too, but I was the only one who became a singer because my late father didn't want his children to be known as singers and he wouldn't allow us to take part in artistic activities. Some singers perform in cabarets and parties, and it was unacceptable to my father that his children (especially his daughters) should become singers. Our family is very moral and religious; this meant that there was an added sensitivity against our entering the world of singing. They told us that anyone with a good voice should perform for his/her own pleasure at home. When I was 10-years-old, I had my first singing lesson from my father. ... After I finished primary school, I went to Tehran to see my sister. And, since I was brimming with the love of singing and I could take singing lessons in Tehran, I never went back to Fuman. When my father heard about my decision he was totally opposed to it. But my sister and her husband supported me. They were the people who really encouraged me.

They say you haven't married yet. Is that true?

Yes, I'm still single. As my favourite singing teacher, the late Ebadi, said to me: 'If you marry, you won't be able to develop your talent.'

What's your advice in terms of making women more active in the field of music?

There is, naturally, a need for greater support and an open climate. Serious decisions must be taken regarding music and the position of women in this field, so that the restrictions imposed on women are removed and Islamic principles safeguarded. It must be possible to advertise in the media and to sell tickets in cultural centres and performance halls [for women's programmes]. A safe environment must be created for women to perform concerts so that women, who form 50 per cent of the population, can see their artists performing. We expect [Islamic guidance and culture minister] Mr Mohajerani to put someone in charge of music who is a committed, knowledgeable and sympathetic artist in his/her own right. When he [Mohajerani] said: 'We will behave in such a way as not to cause the least unhappiness to any artist', this was absolutely what we were hoping for and is the least we can expect. ❏

Edited version of an interview in Zanan *magazine, Iran. Translation by Nilou Mobasser.*

THE GREAT CHALLENGE
The Second International Political Cartoon Exhibition

20 November - 23 December 1998
the.gallery@oxo, Tower Wharf, South Bank, London

The original Great Challenge was laid down in 1958, at the height of the Cold War. The Hungarian Minister of State declared that *"We can, of course use jokes and satire against hostile and reactionary views, but we will not tolerate jokes against socialism."* In response to this, two leading journalists, Josef Josten and Ion Ratiu, challenged cartoonists to prove that they could produce an effective satirical comedy on the totalitarian and paranoid politics of the day. An overwhelming response was received, and the cartoon exhibition toured internationally.

The challenge was re-issued this year by Nicolae and Indrei Ratiu, Ion's sons, and Pat Josten, Josef's widow, and coincides with the 50th anniversary of the Universal Declaration of Human Rights. Again, cartoonists from every continent have risen to the challenge, and have offered a biting commentary on contemporary politics of media domination and censorship. A selection of over 100 new cartoons will be displayed alongside works from 1958, allowing visitors to see social, political and creative changes over the past 40 years. The exhibition promotes the work of Index on Censorship, Amnesty International and the Cartoon Art Trust.

For further details on The Great Challenge, which consists of a programme of talks as well as a free exhibition, call 0171 401 2255.

TIBETAN NUNS

View from Drapchi Prison

Looking from the window,
Seeing nothing but the sky,
The clouds that float in the sky
I wish were my parents

We, the captured friends in spirit,
We might be the ones to fetch the jewel.
No matter how hard we are beaten
Our linked arms cannot be separated

The cloud from the east
Is not a patch that is sewn;
The time will come when the sun
From beneath the clouds shall appear.

I am not sad.
If asked why,
Days will follow days
And the time of release
From here will occur

In October 1993, 14 nuns imprisoned in Lhasa's Drapchi prison for taking part in non-violent pro-independence demonstrations, had their sentences increased to17 years for 'spreading counter-revolutionary propaganda' after they had recorded songs on a tape-recorder smuggled into their cells. Two of the 'singing nuns' are now believed dead. Phuntsog Yangkyi died in 1994 after being beaten for recording the songs. Ngawang Choekyi, 30, is reported to have been one of four nuns who, according to the authorities, committed group suicide by 'stuffing their mouths with scarves'.

RAHIMULLAH YUSUFZAI

All quiet in Kabul

Native guile and the inalienable melody of daily life have postponed the extinction of music in Taliban-held Kabul

Past the last Taliban checkpoint outside Jalalabad, on our way to Kabul, our driver brought out a cassette and snapped it into the tape recorder. It was a film song in Urdu in which a couple reassure one another of their unremitting love. Beside the blue waters of the Kabul river the song had a soothing effect, though the drive along the pot-holed road was back-breaking.

'How can one survive without music, especially in a country that has been at war with itself for two decades,' asked Abdul Saboor, our bearded driver. Saboor played a cat-and-mouse game with Taliban guards during the five-hour drive. Whenever a road-block came into view, the cassette would be slipped into one of his numerous pockets, only to reappear as soon as the danger was past. Then the music would again fill the interior and evaporate into the wild country outside.

Saboor was adept at dodging the guards, but others aren't so lucky. One visible proof was the black and brown streamers hanging from poles and trees. They were the innards of cassettes that had been ripped out and 'hanged' as a reminder to travellers of the ban imposed on music throughout their territory by the Taliban. When, on 27 September 1996, Kabul also fell to the movement, the ban on music and all other forms of electronic entertainment transformed what was once a cosmopolitan city into a virtual ghost town.

Few drivers in the capital take the same risks as Saboor on the deserted and unpoliced Jalalabad-Kabul highway. There are more Taliban here than anywhere else in Afghanistan – hardly surprising, since the forces of former defence minister Ahmad Shah Masood are dug-in only 25km to the north. But the Pashto-speaking Taliban also believe they have to maintain a tight grip in Afghanistan's biggest urban centre to block any challenge from its overwhelmingly Persian-speaking citizens. As Sunni Muslims of the most puritanical kind, they also contend with a significant Shia population.

During the day, Kabul is the quietest city in Asia; by sunset, the bazaars close down as shopkeepers and customers try to reach the safety of their silent homes. The curfew starts at 10pm but, by nightfall, the streets are already deserted except for Hi-Lux pickups, loaded with gunmen from the *Amr Bil Marof Wa Nai Az Munkir* (Office for the Propagation of Virtue and the Prevention of Vice, religious police) looking for violators of Taliban decrees.

The ban has prompted music-lovers to find new means of dodging the restrictions. One ploy is to keep one of the few tolerated cassettes in the vehicle along with those containing the forbidden, instrument-based music. So tapes with recitations from the Quran, *Naats* praising the Prophet Mohammad or Taliban political chants are kept handy to be played at checkpoints. Once out of sight, it is back to the popular Pashto and Persian singers like Nashanas, Ahmad Zahir, Qamar Gulla, Farhad Darya, Farzana, Shah Wali, Abdullah Moquray, Naghma and Mangal.

These artistes and many more abandoned Kabul during the Soviet occupation and flocked to Pakistan. Some have since gone to the West, but the majority remain in Peshawar in Pakistan where they have enriched Pashto music and revived the flagging taste for Persian language and melodies. Singing couples – such as Naghma and Mangal, Aziza Afghan and Ismail Feroz, Parastu and Rahim Mehryar, Hangama and Ahmad Wali – have all earned fame and money through a musical genre that is wholly anathema to the new rulers of Afghanistan.

Taliban officials justify the ban by arguing that music has a corrupting influence on the sexes, distracting them from their real duties: to pray and to praise God. Many rank-and-file believe that those homes where God is most often praised will be most blessed. By the same yardstick, they are of the firm belief that homes and countries where music is played all the time will be cursed.

The ban has not only forced singers out of business: vendors of televisions, videos, musical instruments and tapes have all had to find new livelihoods, a difficult prospect in a stagnant economy. Some, reluctantly, have taken to selling Taliban cassettes, but there is little market. 'How many Taliban cassettes can I sell when only the Taliban buy them?' wondered stall-owner Abdul Jabbar. 'Anyway, every 'Talib' can chant, so what's the point in him buying a cassette with someone else's chanting?'

In the past, cassettes labels showed glamorous pictures of the artists; Taliban-approved cassettes are invariably plastered with images of rifles and rocket-launchers. They not only promote the Taliban's prowess in the battlefield, but fulfil the government injunction that the taking and displaying of pictures of living creatures is 'un-Islamic'.

Those caught with music are reprimanded and their cassettes ripped apart. Some may be admonished with a stick – especially if they try to argue with the guards – and briefly lectured on the 'evils of listening to music'. According to interior minister Mulla Khairullah Khairkhwa, the idea behind the punishment is not to hurt, but 'to reform'.

Our driver Saboor agreed. He wasn't aware of anyone being jailed for keeping or playing a cassette. Still, the ordinary Afghan dreads the *Amr Bil Marof Wa Nai Az Munkir* and it is the fear of being caught by its commander, Mulla Qalamuddin, or his baton-wielding cops that makes most Kabulis think twice before listening to music, even behind the four walls of their homes.

Some families are willing to risk the penalties to listen to their favourite singers, but usually in the air-raid shelters which are a permanent feature of affluent houses after nearly five years of shelling. Some keep their forbidden televisions, VCRs and dish antennas, either in the basement or buried somewhere on their land. In the border provinces, Afghans can spice up their lives by tuning into radio and TV from Pakistan, Uzbekistan, Tajikistan and Turkmenistan. And the same Afghans who grow beards, wear the veil and shun music in their Taliban-ruled homeland, are completely transformed once they cross into any neighbouring country.

The Taliban are mistaken if they believe they have killed music and purified the people of sinful thoughts with their censorship. Even in Kabul, music is still in the air – in the rhymes mothers sing to their children, in the schools where every lesson is taught in the form of rhythmic choruses to make it easier to understand. And the sound of the call to prayer from the loudspeakers on Kabul's mosques is a different kind of music. If not, the Prophet would not have insisted that Hazrat Bilal, the slave with the golden throat, should give the *Azan*, or call for prayer, in Medina as long as he was alive.

Even the monotonous chants that the Taliban proudly sing in praise of their founder, Leader of All The Faithful, Mulla Mohammad Omar, would be unpalatable if they didn't possess some rhyme or reason. ❏

Rahimullah Yusufzai is Afghan correspondent for the BBC Pashto service and a staff reporter on the News, *a Pakistani daily*

OLE REITOV

Rock – a spiritual pollution

A young person's guide to video censorship in Chinese television

If you could watch the pop programmes on Beijing TV (BTV) you would notice a signal difference between the videos show in China and those in Europe or the USA. The absence of the naked back of Sade, for instance, is not because she recorded two different videos, but because the Chinese editor removed that 'not to be shown' part of her anatomy.

'Video censorship is not just a question of the music,' says Li, a young, but experienced TV producer who divides her working time between the mainland and Hong Kong. 'Rock'n'roll is out, but even softer music finds itself in trouble if the performer doesn't look right. Certain areas of the body are more forbidden than others and nudity is not allowed.'

Li is living through what many broadcasters lived through in Europe and the USA in the 1960s: hair is definitely an issue. 'We can't show bands with men with long hair or women who have very short hair, earrings and strange make up. The decision-makers think it conveys a bizarre image that is not good for our young people. Women in Chinese society normally have long hair and if you cut your hair like a monk it is very strange. On the other hand, it is considered 'unhealthy' for men to have hair like women, down to their ears. Nor can we show violent images. This business of censorship is far more about image than music.'

As the person responsible for putting together one of the most popular pop shows on BTV, Li has become expert in replacing 'forbidden' images. If a video has only a few such sequences and the music itself is acceptable, there are easy ways of making it more respectable. 'We just use other shots from the same video and 'repair' the part we have to cut out. It's pretty easy. You have the music, so you just calculate how many seconds you have to cut and you replace that part with acceptable images.

Li is caught between her own wide ranging musical tastes and the fact that she must, nevertheless, act as a pre-censor. 'In the beginning, I always asked why we couldn't show this and why we couldn't play that. Six months later, I knew exactly which rhythms were 'strange' and which videos had to be 'repaired'. I go on trying to widen the scope but I never have the final say. After a preview, my boss decides what can and can't be broadcast and the record companies go along with our editing on the videos.

What exactly is 'healthy' music? Li recalls a discussion with a colleague. 'The song in question was a rather gentle ballad, nothing heavy, but she told me it couldn't be played. I asked why and she said, "The meaning of the song is not very healthy." So I replied: "Healthy depends on how you define health." This song is about confusion; it is asking questions. But that was not what we were taught in school; we were told we shouldn't be confused. We could ask questions but we were expected to find a way of working things out.'

In the USA, rock music has been accused of 'moral pollution'; in China the term most often used is 'spiritual pollution'. And anything that is 'SP' is out. 'Maybe rock'n'roll isn't exactly the solution to young, urban Chinese's questions about life, but since we have so little opportunity to express our doubts and criticisms, rock has become synonymous with the 'spiritually polluted'. Controversial rock icon Cui Jian is one artist to whom Li would like to give more scope. 'His songs have affected a whole generation. What he is singing about is what a whole generation has been thinking about: breaking some of the traditional rules and singing about freedom on a personal level.

In Hong Kong, where she works with a rock programme, Li has no problems: 'I can present Chinese rock bands; I can show the long hair and they can say whatever they want – well they can't swear – but in BTV we have to be more careful how they answer questions as well as about their image. Before we interview them we brief them so that they know the rules. It's important for them too: if they break the rules we cut the show.'

After airing what she thought was an entirely uncontroversial Chinese folk singer, Aijing, in a concert from Tokyo during the winter of 1996, Li's show was axed for a month. The programme was cut because the singer jumped around on stage. 'She normally sits down quietly and plays gentle songs. This time she just jumped about on stage a bit, very gently, and my bosses said this was rock. It wasn't and we were all depressed. I considered quitting but decided to keep fighting. ❏

OR

CHEN SHIZHENG

The fate of Tang Xianzu

Even 400-year-old classics can still offend delicate sensibilities

Following a farcical series of self criticisms reminiscent of the Cultural Revolution, the long awaited revival of a 400-year-old classical opera, in rehearsal at Shanghai's glittering new Kunju Theatre, was called off by the Shanghai Bureau of Culture. It accused the director of introducing 'archaic, superstitious and pornographic' elements into his production and vetoed its export first to New York and subsequently to France, Australia and Hong Kong.

Mu Dan Ting, (Peony Pavilion), a masterpiece of Chinese opera written by Tang Xianzu in 1598 during the Ming Dynasty, tells the story of Du Liniang, who meets her ideal lover only in dreams while sleeping in the Peony Pavilion. Only after her death, her love still unrequited, does her dream lover Liu Mengmei arrive in person to encounter her ghost. Liu's true love restores her to life and after many vicissitudes they are united as man and wife.

The opera has not been performed in its entire 55 act, 22-hour-long version since it was written during the Ming dynasty. Under the communists, it was completely written out of the classical repertoire and branded 'feudal, superstitious and pornographic'. But this time, if the director is to be believed, its banning has more to do with political manoevring than the nature of the opera itself.

Even in its day, the opera was seen as anti-feudal and anti-Confucian, extolling the virtues of individual freedom and choice, and speedily incurred the emperor's wrath. In celebration of its four hundreth anniversary, New York's Lincoln Centre and the Kunju Opera House, contracted for a new production of the opera to open the Lincoln Centre Festival in July 1998. But things went suddenly and drastically wrong. ❏

Yang Lian talks to the director Chen Shizheng

Yang Lian: *Are you surprised by what's happened to the* Peony Pavilion*?*
Chen Shizheng: Yes and no. I've lived outside China for so long one forgets. But this is China, I should have expected something like this.

Is there a contradiction between China's economic reform and this Maoist-style drama?

This lopsided combination of economic reform with the same old autocratic politics has only one logic: to crush any independent thought; one goal: to sustain the powers that be. From the official viewpoint, they are complementary not contradictory. Even though the Cultural Revolution ended over 20 years ago, the style of their 'criticisms' of my production is proof that the methods of control have not changed.

They say you have 'sullied' the reputation of one of China's greatest classics. What exactly were you trying to achieve artistically?

I wanted to convey my personal interpretation or understanding of the *Peony Pavilion* in its entirety. In China, when they talk about a 'traditional' performance what they actually mean is an 'official' performance. This unchanging, dead tradition becomes just another version of state ideology. I wanted to inject it with the living power of folk culture: to break down the boundary between theatre and reality; between stage and audience; art and life; the classical language of the text and everyday speech. For instance, the audience can actually see the actors putting on their make-up and the musicians who accompany the performance are no longer hidden. Like the famous Sung scroll, 'Life on

Behind the scenes at the opera: a glimpse denied – Credit: Rex/Skyline

the river during Qing Ming', that is, as it were, a 'documentary' of life 1,000 years ago, this performance, all 22 hours of it, should reflect life outside the theatre as well as in; people should feel they are participating in the piece.

Since it was written 400 years ago, the opera has never been performed in its entirety. Tang Xianzu, acclaimed as one of our greatest classical writers – the 'Shakespeare of China' – has seen his works butchered and manipulated since the day he wrote them, in particular this piece. This is not just a love story as so many think, it's about humanity's quest for personal escape from the constraints of a rigid and repressive society. About the loneliness of the one who awakes while others still sleep. The *Peony Pavilion* was progressively cut from its original 55 acts, to 24 acts; today only four or five are left – and they've all been rewritten. I'm the first director who has ever tried to show Tang Xianzu's true face to the public. Of course this doesn't suit the official traditionalists.

The 400 year solitude of Tang Xianzu is not over.

He is not alone in his solitude: today I have joined him. We are one.

What do you feel about being banned in the name of tradition?

Tradition can only stay alive if it is constantly renewed, recreated through personal reinterpretation. Tang Xianzu's play and my direction intersect at the point of our separate and individual self expression. It's because of this we both suffer the same fate. This Shanghai Cultural Bureau told me: 'You are not allowed to reinterpret Chinese culture.' All I was doing was offering a personal view, not speaking for the whole of China. What they meant was: 'Only we have the right to represent Chinese culture – to determine what it is and it is not. What they want is a colourful fake, like their fake 'antiques' made for export: a 'Made in China' export version of the *Peony Pavilion* to adorn their new economic prosperity. The face of reformed China. Like the annual kitsch 'Spring Festival Party' for mass consumption on state-run CCTV. As the Saying of Chairman Mao goes: 'Art serves politics.' 'Tradition' also.

So political power is still the controlling value?

The death of classical Chinese opera; the new life my production has infused into it; the fact that actors who are going through a very tough time had the chance to make a decent living; breaking the contract agreed with the USA: all these are as nothing compared to their fear of losing control.

How do the higher echelons of authority see all this?

They praised the head of the Shanghai Cultural Bureau for his vigilance in preventing something that would have given a 'bad impression' of China from getting out.

So what's the real problem with the production?

An individual has challenged authority and its 'closed' view of culture; those in power have suppressed both the personal interpretation and the concept of an 'open' culture. The only real injury is to Chinese culture: any hope of infusing it with real life has been cut off. The blind obedience instilled in the Cultural Revolution and the cruel massacre in Tiananmen Square demonstrated that there would be no place for freedom of thought or expression. The banning of this work shows they have learned nothing from the past. They are still hacking away at people's creative expression. Creativity is the life blood of any culture

And the fate of Tang Xianzu?

Nothing, including culture, will change until the whole political structure is changed. Tang Xianzu is doomed to go on waiting. ❏

Yang Lian *is a Chinese poet exiled in London. His next petry collection,* Where the sea stands still *will be published by Bloodaxe Books, UK, in January 1999*

news

Singing of alien tongues
John Kamau

The state-run Kenya Broadcasting Corporation (KBC) bans songs in any of the country's 40-plus vernacular languages from its two national services. The blacklist was imposed 12 years ago when then radio boss Cornelius Nyamboki insisted musicians sing in either Swahili or English to curb the rise of 'ethnic nationalism'. It didn't affect languages used beyond Kenya's borders: 75 per cent of the national playlist are in the Lingala of former Zaire, while Swahili lyrics now chip in a mere 20 per cent.

Local language songs can be played during 'specialist' programmes, such as *Muziki asili wa Kenya* ('Traditional Music of Kenya'), but they allocated less than one hour a day. KBC's regional stations do play lyrics in local tongues, but reception is poor.

In spite of the ban, Nairobi jukeboxes feature hits in Kikuyu, the language of Kenya's largest ethnic group, while River Road has become a raucous Tin Pan Alley. But when Kikuyu stars, four years ago, tried to break the boycott by singing in Swahili, they received no better reception.

The songs were blacklisted because they were sung 'with a River Road accent'.

OLE REITOV

Music and identity

The director of information was a powerful man. Not only did he control the future of the media in Bhutan, but as permanent secretary to the more or less feudal King Jigme, his word was often seen as the royal command.

So when the director told the young producers that the programme they had produced on music in Bhutan could not be broadcast, they knew what that meant. The director went on to explain why: the programme, he said, was 'not in line with the country's cultural and linguistic policy'.

So what was their 'crime? By going onto the streets of Thimphu, the capital of Bhutan, and asking young and old a simple question, 'What kind of music do you listen to?' the producers had done nothing more than reflect the reality of a multilingual country with few but strong cultural and linguistic influences from neighbouring India and Tibet.

The answers came as no surprise to anyone: drivers, tea-house guests, youngsters and shopkeepers listened to a mixture of traditional Bhutanese folk tunes, Hindi songs from the Bollywood film factory and the odd western pop tune. They tuned-in to the Bhutan Broadcasting Service or All India Radio and bought the limited number of counterfeit cassettes in the bazaar.

Nor was it surprising that the 'common people' being interviewed spoke the official national Dzongkha language with English or Nepali words thrown in. Very few people in Bhutan master the national language completely.

And that was what the trouble was all about: the director didn't like this mixture of music and languages in the national programme. English music and the English language in the English national service was OK; the Nepali language and Nepali music in the Nepalese service was equally acceptable. But no multicultural blend please.

As a UNESCO consultant to Bhutan's radio service and an advisor to the young producers, I had to weigh respect for international development funding and human rights against the risk of a conflict with the director. Since the director made no approach to me, we went on with the programme. Though never in the open, the conflict was on.

For a small country like Bhutan, more or less isolated for centuries from the onslaught of foreign cultural influences, the desire to protect their culture is understandable. Neighbouring Nepal, with its massive tourist industry, is hardly a role model for the protection of the national heritage. But the dividing line between 'protectionism' and 'chauvinism' is a narrow one and the director of information was a hard-line nationalist propagating the strict national dress and 'manners' codes. Where UNESCO declarations and human rights documents speak of minority rights, the Bhutanese would talk of national rights: that is to say the right of the king to tell others what to the wear and how to behave.

The positive aspect of this was the protection of an ancient civilisation; the down side was the suppression of people's cultural rights. No foreign music in the national language service, please.

But my Bhutanese colleagues and I had a different problem. what exactly is the national music of Bhutan? And when is any development of their songs going to be accepted as Bhutanese? Most of the instruments used in Bhutan's traditional music come from Tibet, many of the songs are shared with its Tibetan neighbours and the former director of the national music troupe was a Tibetan. The director does not like the use of western instruments in traditional music nor does he favour any form of 'modernisation'.

Dogged by such isolationism, Bhutanese music stands no chance of developing a modern national identity that, like the Bhutanese themselves, stands any chance of resisting the growing encroachments of the outside world on their feudal kingdom. ❏

Ole Reitov

CRASS

Bata Motel

europe

I've got 54321
I've got a red pair of high-heels on
Tumble me over, it doesn't take much
Tumble me over, tumble me, push
In my red high-heels I've no control
The rituals of repression are so old
You can do what you like, there'll be no reprisal
I'm yours, yes I'm yours, it's my means of survival

Well today I look so good
Just like I know I should
My breasts to tempt inside my bra
My face is painted like a movie star
I've studied my flaws in your reflection
And put them to rights with savage correction
I've turned my statuesque perfection
And shone it over in your direction
So come on darling, make me yours
Trip me over, show me the floor
Tease me, tease me, make me stay
In my red high-heels I can't get away
I'm trussed and bound like an oven ready bird
But I bleed without dying and I won't say a word
Slice my flesh and I'll ride the scar
Put me into gear like your lady car
Drive me fast and crash me crazy
I'll rise from the wreckage as fresh as a daisy
These wounds leave furrows as they heal
I've travelled them, they're red and real
I know them well they're part of me
My birth, my sex, my history
They grew with me, my closest friend
My pain's my own, my pain's my end
Clip my wings so you know where I am
I can't get lost while you're my man
Tame me so I know your call
I've stabbed my heels so I am tall
I've bound my twisted falling fall
Beautiful mute against the wall
Beautifully mutilated as I fall

Excerpt from Bata Motel. Lyric by Crass. See disc notes p8/9

AHMED BURIC

Marriage made in Hell

The fusion of folk and funk – of glamour with violence – triggered a wave of Balkan hate music with its roots back in World War II

In the summer of 1993, when CD and tape pirates in Zagreb's Ban Jelacic Square sold all 20,000 copies of Unprofor Big Band's latest album, it was obvious that Balkan pop culture had entered a new era – the Years of Loathing.

The album cover showed a monkey with an automatic rifle and wearing a UN peace-keeping helmet. Called 'Fuck Them All', the fuck-word was written in Cyrillic, though the band was Croatian. The songs blamed Serbs and the international community for both the war and Croatia's losses, then badly sapping the nation's morale. One track was dedicated to the then hard-line Bosnian Serb nationalist leader Biljana Plavsic, whom the West championed in the 1998 elections as the region's key moderate: 'Biljana you should know you won't be a lady/ You'll eat hard-corn mush/ You motherfucker!' The song has never officially been banned, but nor has it been aired on state-run radio stations. However, local stations, particularly ones close to the front lines, played it remorselessly.

With a population of 25 million, Yugoslavia had a highly sophisticated pop scene for a socialist country. Performers routinely sold up to one million copies of their discs. The national states that followed the break-up had far smaller markets and Croatia was probably in the worst position to adapt to the new realities. Ever since the early 1990s, anything remotely echoing Serbian folk had been eliminated from its public broadcasting. In Serbia, the policy was different: radio stations

AHMED BURIC

aired practically everything, except for the songs of artists most openly aligned with Croatian, Slovenian or Bosnian independence.

In Bosnian territories controlled by Serbia and Croatia, pop music mirrored the situations in those countries. Though not entirely free of a certain nationalist euphoria, Bosnian music remained relatively uninfected by chauvinism.

It was the Serb musicians who undoubtedly went furthest down the road of wartime hate songs. One instance is the 1992 number by folk stars the Brothers Bajic. Dedicated to German Foreign Minister Hans Dietrich Genscher, the first to recognise Croatian independence, it goes: 'Hey Bosche Genscher/Genscher/Are you having dinner at Tudjman's?' As the war intensified, Baja Mali Kninja, a 13-year-old artist from the Serbian town of Knin in Croatia, serenaded Bosnian President Alija Izetbegovic thus: 'I don't like you Alija/You've destroyed the Serbian dream/I hope 100 *mujahedin* drown every day in the Drina.'

As sanctions hit Serbia in 1992, the airwaves were dominated by a song that claimed: 'Nobody can harm us/We are stronger than destiny/Those who don't like us /Can only hate us.' A folk song about a shepherd driving his sheep across the river was recast with the sheep replaced by 'Croatian fascist *Ustashis*'. Pope John Paul II was celebrated for his condemnation of Serbian war crimes with: 'Hey Pope, Pope/I wonder what God you worship/You hate the Serbs/You hate the Serbs/ All the others you love.'

Serbian society was flooded by 'folk' propaganda as the black economy eulogised a fast life of partying and crime. Extra Nina, one female pop arriviste, released a song in 1993 with the refrain: 'Coca-Cola, Marlboro, Suzuki/Discos, guitars, *bouzouki*/That's life, it's not a TV ad/Nobody does as well as we.'

A new romance in Serbia's gangster high society splashed across the front pages in 1996 when its most popular folk singer, Svetlana Ceca Velickovic, married Zeljko Raznatovic Arkan, commander of the Tigers armed militia, a reported war criminal and probably the most powerful man in Yugoslavia this decade after President Slobodan Milosevic. He is also wanted by Interpol in connection with a series of bank robberies in the EU.

Arkan's pariah status abroad has not undermined his reputation as one of the greatest figures of his time at home. Fifteen hundred guests attended the 'super-marriage', either because they could not – or dared

150   INDEX ON CENSORSHIP 6 1998

not – refuse. It was a gala occasion, accompanied by a concert with some of Serbia's most popular folk artists. The wedding video became a major hit, bonding Ceca's showbiz glamour with Arkan's intimidating muscle.

The paradoxes of Balkan nationalism can be best illustrated by two anecdotes connected to the Arkan-Ceca video. Surprisingly, it sold well among Bosnians: in the divided city of Mostar, the latter would play it at maximum volume to annoy their Croat enemies across the Neretva river. Even while battling the Serbs from their trenches, Bosnian troops would listen to Ceca in a maudlin reverie – even as her husband was burying their comrades and Croat allies.

Patriot songs married kitsch with a species of mass hysteria. The mix of traditional folk with what was called 'Turbo-folk' – a blend of techno, trance and funk – spawned a new lifestyle in rationed, wartime Serbia. Men with cropped hair, gold chains and sweat-shirts tried to look dangerous as they circulated with 'sponsored girls', in expensive fur and jewellery, who were expected to dance wildly in the 'folkotheques', where the 'Turbo folk' hung out.

In Croatia, too, folk and techno joined forces. Between 1992 and 1995, audiences were flooded by a fusion of Dinaric and Herzegovinian folk – known as *gange* in the rural areas – and hard rock, a retro, heavy-metal guitar sound mixed with synthesised drums. This was the launchpad for the most extreme hate music from artists like Marko Perkovic. In one of his videos, a uniformed Perkovic – nicknamed 'Thompson' after the sub-machine gun – appeared alongside Croatian soldiers singing: 'Hey, you Serbian volunteers/You Chetnik scum/You will not escape/Not even in Serbia.' His second album is even more to the point: 'Because of Anica and a jug of wine/I will set Krajina on fire/All the way to Knin/I'll set on fire two or three Serbian headquarters/I haven't come for nothing.' One of the few songs officially banned in Croatia was Thompson's remix of an old *Ustashi* number in which he promises to ford the Drina and torch Serbia.

Wartime nationalism in Serbia and Croatia produced music that would have been unthinkable under Tito's regime. Censorship, which had prohibited nationalism in the public sphere, had vanished together with communism. Nationalist 'folk' was a logical follow-up to the *Ustashi* and *Chetnik* propaganda songs of World War II, many of which, extolling the virtues of their heroes slain by Tito's partisans who 'stole the country', were still being smuggled into the country in the 1970s and 1980s. By the time the war started in 1991, musicians who wanted to survive had to take up the prevailing social discourse – nationalism and victory. Those who did not have the stomach for it changed profession, hid, or tried to find work abroad. Darko Rundek, founder of the influential Haustor band, explained how he felt: 'I was at Ban Jelacic Square and I saw people chanting vile, fascist slogans. The next morning I packed and left for Paris. Now, when I came to Zagreb, I feel they want to impose Franjo Tudjman on us as the father of the nation. I don't need a third father. My biological father and God are good enough for me.' ❑

Ahmed Buric is a freelance journalist based in Sarajevo. He is currently reviewing theatre, film, and books for Dani *magazine and* Oslobodjenje

AUSTRALIA

Election notes
Andrew Elkin

For an independent candidate in Australia, a gimmick can go a long way. Gay lecturer Simon Hunt changed his name to 'Pauline Pantsdown', became the drag lookalike of One Nation Party figurehead Pauline Hanson and turned into an overnight pop sensation. His manifesto? The installation of 'homosexual government' – and the humiliation of Hanson. 'I'm a Backdoor Man', Pantsdown's song, flew into the charts, but was banned on 28 September following an injunction taken out by Pauline Hanson a month earlier. Pantsdown created the song by putting Hanson's own words – though not in the order she used them – to a pop beat and into the mouth of a gay man.
Pantsdown immediately set to work on 'I Don't Like It', which also hit number one. Hanson did not challenge the new hit, but spent the last weeks of her campaign locked in a verbal battle with her sequinned alter ego. 'I told her to tone down her makeup,' said Pantsdown, 'but she wouldn't listen'. Hanson lost heavily in her own constituency and One Nation took just one seat in the 3 October election.
'That's not good for my character continuing,' Pantsdown commented, 'but it's best for the greater good.'

HELENE LOOW

White Noise

Neo-Nazi groups are recruiting throughout the developed world; leading the drive are their high energy, punk-derived anthems of hate

E very revolutionary movement, has its own music, lyrics and poets. They neither create nor lead the revolution; they articulate its dreams, visions and fantasies of the utopian society pursued by the movement.

The modern racist propagandist is not, as in the 1930s, a party strategist or skilled speaker, but a combination of rock star and street fighter. It's no longer a question of music for national socialists or racists, the music itself has become the ideology. The choreography of 'White Noise' concerts makes it evident that the singer, strutting heiratically across the stage, is the high priest of a ritual celebration, the leader controlling the public as did his Nazi forbears.

White Noise music and the extreme racist and xenophobic counter-culture has grown during the past 10 years, particularly among the generation born in the 1960s and 1970s. Along with 'separatist rock', it came to Sweden in the late 70s and early 80s when the anti-immigration organisation *Bevara Sverige Svenskt* (BSS: Keep Sweden Swedish) started to distribute audio tapes labelled 'Music for Patriots'.

Throughout its early years, the movement and its musical arm suffered from an acute lack of finance. But by 1995, its poor quality home-made tapes and shabby photocopied newsletters had been replaced by a thriving recording industry dedicated to the production and sale of White Noise. Together with the mail order companies that sell the goods, it provides the sound financial base for the growing underground culture of white power.

The moving spirit behind this is Lars Magnus Westrup, founder in

1993 of Ragnarock Records, and backed financially by handful of nationalist businessmen and activists. Westrup, had a long history of activism in various national socialist, fascist and extreme nationalist groups. During World War II, he was a member of the national socialist organisation *Sveaborg*, but left after the war for Franco's Spain, where he founded and ran a Swedish radio station on Majorca. On Franco's death, he returned to Sweden to become secretary of its extreme right-wing party *Framstegspartiet* (Progressive Party).

Westrup started in business in a modest way by selling tapes of Rudolf Hess speeches and the poetry of the Swedish fascist leader Per Engdahl. With the creation of Ragnarock Records he hit the big time. Westrup died in May 1995, but in 1996, Ragnarock Records founded *Wasakåren* for 'the promotion of genuine Swedish music'.

The production and distribution of propaganda material grew rapidly in the early-90s with the proliferation of mail-order companies and stores, selling White Noise paraphernalia – music, NS and racist literature, books on the Vikings and their pagan religious cults (Asatro), T-shirts, stickers, armlets, banners and insignia, videos, uniforms, magazines, posters, jewellery and so on. In 1994, *Nordland*, Scandinavia's leading White Noise magazine, mail-order and record company made its appearance.

Sweden's first White Noise concert was in 1985, when the UK group Skrewdriver played in Stockholm. Since then, groups and concerts have proliferated. In April 1994, the largest NS demonstration since 1945 took place in the small town of Alingsås, near Gothenburg. Between 500 and 600 demonstrators from Sweden, Norway, Denmark and Germany marched from the town to a concert with *Totenkopf*, *Svastica*, 'No Remorse' and the Welsh group 'Celtic Warriors'. It was the starting point of a series of large concerts throughout Sweden, and gave a boost to the formation of Swedish White Noise rock groups such as Division S, Vit Aggression, *Bärsärkarna*, *Enhärjarna*, Odins Änglar and *Dirlewanger*, linked to the racist counter-culture across Europe, notably in the UK, Germany and Scandinavia, and in the USA.

In 1996, in response to accusations of incitement to racial hatred made by the Swedish Committee against anti-Semitism to the Chancellor of Justice, Ragnarock made the following statement:

'Ragnarock records and its artists do not encourage their customers or listeners to use violence or hatred towards individual migrants or ethnic minorities, but to combat the anti-Swedish politicians who use mass immigration as a mean to exterminate the Swedish people and the Swedish culture. To protect your own people, your culture or nation is not racial hatred.'

Nordland responded to the reports filed by the committee by pointing out that the lead singer in the punk group *Stockholm's Negrer* (Stockholm's niggers) – nowadays spokesman for the state-organised Youth against Racism, financed by the ministry of civil affairs – had, in 1986, received similar complaints for texts like 'Bloody Swedes, move out/We also live here you blond blue-eyed beautiful creep/Death to all blond bloody Vikings/What the devil! How I hate you'. Claiming 'freedom of artistic expression', he was cleared of all charges. Nordland, however, added that they were well aware that equality before the law did not apply to them, and concluded; 'Even when our enemies are badmouthing us and our views, they can no longer deny that the music is unique and talented and that our ideals are presented in an attractive and intelligent fashion.'

Reports from the Swedish committee also led to charges against the owner of Svea Music for distributing and selling the album 'White Solidarity'. Only one track, by the Finnish group Mistreat was found guilty of incitement to racial hatred. To date, this is the only conviction against White Noise. ❑

Heléne Lööw is a member of Sweden's National Council for Crime Prevention

MARK LUDWIG

Tales of Terezín

The Nazis used music as a propaganda tool in the service of its doctrine of racial purity and superiority. Composers and musicians who did not fit the formula found themselves in the camps

In the 1920s, Weimar Germany was home to a rich and diverse mix of artistic and political movements. Composers stretched the boundaries of, and in some cases charted new courses for, classical music. *Zeitmusik* (music of the time), the 12 tone system and jazz were part of a new and excitingly diverse web of musical movements. As Hitler and the Nazi Party assumed control of Germany, the arts and the political climate were affected. Under the Nazi dictatorship, the arts – particularly music – were used as tools for indoctrinating and controlling the German nation with an ideology of national superiority, suppression and racial hatred.

Entartete Musik was the name given by the Nazis to a wide variety of composers and musical genres as part of their propaganda machine. *Entartete* – 'degenerate', connotating psychologically abnormal behaviour – signified something abnormal about the art that was perceived as a threat to German society. The initial introduction of this concept to the public was through an exhibit of visual arts in Munich in 1937. The following year in Dusseldorf, music received similar attention in the *Entartete Musik* exhibition.

The Nazis planned to use music, as well as other arts, as a political tool to unify and educate the racially pure German Volk. In addition to educating people about the dangers of degenerate music, the public was also 'protected' from cultural pollution by a ban on the performance, recording and publication of this music.

The music targeted was enormously varied, as were the lives of the

Entartete
MUSIK
EINE ABRECHNUNG VON
STAATSRAT Dr. H.S. ZIEGLER

composers. What it had in common were either elements of jazz, atonal music or, most specifically, any music written by Jewish composers. Racial considerations aside, the music of many German composers who were experimenting with new musical forms was also targeted. In this twisted formula, this music was symptomatic of a cancer infecting German culture. The Nazi propaganda ministry wanted to educate the public about its danger and to revitalize the concept of a pure German music as exemplified by Wagner and Bruckner. Ironically, many people attended the 1938 *Entartete Musik* exhibition in the hope of hearing Kurt Weill, one of the 'degenerate' composers.

The *Entartete* programme became a policy of censorship that supported the ethnic and political cleansing of German society. Some of the targeted musicians were able to leave: composers such as Schoenberg, Toch, Hindemith, Waxman and Korngold came to the USA to make new lives for themselves. Others were not so fortunate: many exceptionally gifted artists were imprisoned and eventually murdered.

A number of these artists were among the western European Jewish intelligentsia sent to the Theresienstadt (Terezín) concentration camp just north of Prague. The camp functioned both as a transit camp to the Nazi death camps and as a propaganda vehicle designed to deceive the world community about the true nature of the 'Final Solution'. One hundred and twenty thousand people passed through Terezín; 33,000 died in the camp. Of the 87,000 who were sent on to death camps, only five per cent survived. Terezín was labeled a 'paradise ghetto' by the Nazis. However, the lack of adequate medical care, overcrowding, starvation and torture made living conditions intolerable. Before the war Terezín was a Czech garrison town with a population of approximately 6,000; converted into a concentration camp, Terezín's population peaked at over 58,000.

Remarkably, despite the horror of the living conditions inside the camp, by a variety of ingenious means musical instruments were smuggled into Terezín as early as the second transport. One group of prisoners brought a cello into the camp wrapped like a corpse. They reported the instrument (deceased) as a death during the transport to Terezín.

At first, concerts were held secretly in the attics and basements of the barracks. The performances increased with the growing number of

'Film and Reality' by Fritz Taussig – Credit: Terezín Chamber Music Foundation Archives

amateur and professional artists arriving with each transport. This active cultural community included many of Europe's most gifted artists, musicians and literary figures. Upon discovery of these secret performances, the Nazis realized the importance of culture to the lives of the prisoners in Theresienstadt and initially permitted such cultural activities, believing this to be another measure with which to control the ghetto population with minimal forces. The Nazis would later manipulate these activities as the tide of the war changed. In June 1944, select performances by the prisoners were used for propaganda purposes to counter evidence and reports of 'atrocities' filtering to the Allies.

In 1942, the *Freizeit-Gestaultung* – the Administration for Free Time Activities – was instituted by the Nazi SS command. Evolving from the *Kameradschaftsabend*, the *Freizeit-Gestaultung* was a Jewish–run organization responsible for a wide range of activities offered to the prisoners, including lectures, sports, chess, theatre, cabaret, opera, jazz and chamber concerts. Professional and amateur musicians were recruited by the Council of Elders to administer musical events for the prisoners. The music division of the *Freizeit-Gestaultung* was responsible for rehearsal scheduling and concert programming, in addition to the acquisition of musical instruments and supplies.

It also distributed tickets for all events in Theresienstadt. A block of tickets were usually reserved for Theresienstadt 'prominents', prisoners who had distinguished themselves professionally before their incarceration or were connected with the Council of Elders. While most tickets were free, some were exchanged for 'Terezín Ghetto vouchers' issued by the camp labour units. All these cultural activities were only a brief escape from the hardships of Theresienstadt and the constant fear of being placed on a transport, sent away from their family and friends and ultimately to their death.

Four composers emerged as the central creative forces in this extraordinary cultural community; Gideon Klein, Pavel Haas, Hans Krása and Viktor Ullmann. Former students of Arnold Schoenberg, Alois Haba, Alexander Zemlinsky and Leos Janacek, these composers were among the significant forces shaping classical music in their generation. In the 1920s and 1930s, their compositions were premiered by orchestras in Europe and the USA (most notably the Philadelphia Orchestra and Boston Symphony Orchestra) under the direction of George Szell, William Steinberg, Leopold Stokowski and Serge

Poster for Hans Krása opera 'Brundibar' – Credit: Terezín Chamber Music Foundation Archives

HANS KRÁSA

FLAŠINETÁŘ

Brundibár

DĚTSKÁ OPERA O 2 OBRAZECH

Hudebně nastudoval
A ŘÍDÍ: RUDOLF FREUDENFELD
Režie a scéna: Fr. Zelenka
TANEČNÍ SPOLUPRÁCE KAMILA ROSENBAUMOVÁ
Zpívají, hrají a tančí
DĚTI TEREZÍNSKÝCH DĚTSKÝCH ÚTULKŮ

Koussevitsky.

In an attempt to portray Theresienstadt to the outside world as a 'paradise ghetto' for the Jews, the Nazis forced the prisoners to perform works by these composers. A performance of Hans Krása's children's opera *Brundibar* (originally composed in Prague in 1939) was staged at Theresienstadt during a visit by an International Red Cross Committee on 23 June 1944; scenes from the opera were shown in the Nazi propaganda film *Der Fuhrer schenkt den Juden eine Stadt* (The Fuhrer Gives the Jews a City). This film also included a sham performance of Pavel Haas's *Study for String Orchestra*. Conductor and musicians are seen to acknowledge the applause of an audience comprising Theresienstadt prisoners. The camera focuses on Haas in the audience as the narrator comments: 'Musical performances are happily attended by all. The work of a Jewish composer in Theresienstadt is performed.'

Placed on the last transports from Theresienstadt to the East in October 1944, both Haas and Krása died in the gas chambers of Auschwitz.

Before the Nazi occupation of Czechoslovakia, Viktor Ullmann was establishing a promising career as a composer and conductor. A student and conducting assistant to Alexander Zemlinsky during the 1920s, Ullmann had access to the social and professional circle of Arnold Schoenberg. Unlike Schoenberg and Zemlinsky, Ullmann was unable to leave Europe before the outbreak of World War II. He was deported to Terezín on 8 September 1942. Perhaps the most important work he composed in Terezín was his opera *Der Kaiser von Atlantis*. The libretto was by Petr Kien, a young poet and painter also incarcerated in Theresienstadt. The text is an allegory on the nature of fascism and the low value it places on life. Ullmann drew from an array of musical sources, mixing elements of musical parody and cabaret with references to Bach, Suk and Mahler. The pervasive leitmotif for the opera quotes the death motif from Suk's *Asrael Symphony*.

Rehearsals for the opera were held in the summer of 1944. The grotesque distortion of *Deutschland uber alles* in the opera's first scene is likely to have provoked the Nazi's decision to prevent performances in Terezín, one of the few instances where they exerted any censorship of music in the camp. On 16 October 1944, Ullmann, his son Max and his wife were sent to Auschwitz. They died in the gas chambers on 18 October 1944.

Mark Ludwig is the director and founder of the Terezín Chamber Music Foundation dedicated to assuring the permanence of the music written by composers who perished in the Holocaust. He is a member of the Hawthorne String Quartet and in 1994, produced and directed the exhibition and concert/lecture series 'Silenced Voices: Music Banned by the Nazis'. In November 1997, he launched the MusicFOR/Sarajevo project to rebuild the Music Academy of Sarajevo: www.musicfor.org

PAKISTAN

Two into one won't go
ARIF AZAD

The group Junoon (Obsession) habitually falls foul of the Pakistani authorities, who construe any talk of reunification between India and Pakistan as 'belittling the concept of the ideology of Pakistan', or disagreeing with 'national opinion'. Led by Salman Ahmed, Junoon belt out songs with a socio-political content. A hit about corrupt politicians in September 1996 was swiftly barred from the official airwaves. In September 1997 Pakistan Television broadcast a live Junoon show which so vexed Prime Minister Nawaz Sharif that he sulkily banned jeans and long hair from the national channels. On two recent visits to India, Junoon sang that music had the power to tear down the walls erected on both sides of the border, rounding the message out with the declaration: 'We have no nationality'. That innocuous taunt prompted a full-scale investigation by Pakistan's Council of Arts and Janoon is now the subject of a nationwide ban at home. At a time when the 'Talibanisation' of Pakistan is proceeding apace, the suppression of music with attitude could be the first step on the road to absolute silence.

DONALD KENRICK

Wings of sorrow

One of the most familiar sounds in the fashionable world of café society in the years between the wars was the strain of Gypsy bands who entertained in bars and restaurants across Europe

Once the Nazis came to power in Germany, they systematically set about silencing the sound of Romany music – at least in public places. From February 1936, such performances were banned in Düsseldorf; other towns followed. In 1938, the owner of a restaurant in Cologne who engaged a Romany band was threatened with the loss of his licence, while in the same year in Bremen, a concert planned by a Romany youth group was declared to be 'not of an artistic nature' and the tickets had to bear an additional 'entertainments tax'. The following year, the National Association of Professional Musicians expelled a large number of Romanies and the economics minister ordered police to confiscate the pedlar's licence of any itinerant musician.

Once imprisoned in the early labour camps, however, Romanies and Sinti Romanies were enrolled in camp 'orchestras'. Their music accompanied executions and the sounds of beatings and they entertained SS officers and their VIP guests. In these instances, the music was German, but for their personal entertainment the SS favoured the supposedly traditional Gypsy music played in cafés, now virtually banned outside the camps. They also played to fellow prisoners for small gifts of food, or to keep up their spirits.

The Buchenwald orchestra was formed at the end of 1938 on the order of Deputy Camp Commander Major Rodl. Inmate Ernst Kogon recounts: 'It was ghastly to hear the Romanies strike up their merry marches while exhausted prisoners carried their dead and dying comrades into the camp, or to listen to the music accompanying the whippings.' He recalls one rare occasion the Romanies played for

themselves. 'I shall never forget that icy New Year's Eve of 1939 ...
Suddenly the sound of a Romany violin drifted out from one of the
barracks far off, as though from happier times and climes – tunes from
the Hungarian steppe, melodies from Vienna and Budapest, songs from
home.'

It was to the strains of their own music that Romanies were led off to
their deaths in Jasenovac, the fascist *Ustashi* camp in Croatia. In June
1942, the Romanies and other players were ordered to put on a concert.
The next morning they were murdered. Most Romanies were, however,
killed on arrival. They were marched off from the transports, ordered to
sing wedding songs or a song dedicated to the fascist chief himself –
'Blessed be Pavelic's head' – on their way to the fields where ditches had
already been dug to receive their bodies.

On one occasion a group of Romany musicians in Jasenovac were
asked by the *Ustashi*:

'Do you know "*Hej Slaveni*"?'

'Of course, we know it.'

'Play it!'

The Romanies began to play, unaware that this was the Partisan
hymn.

'The abyss of Hell threatens to no avail/powerless is the flame of
lightning...'

They were told to bring their instruments with them for a concert
over the river in Gradina which, unknown to them, had been set aside as
an extermination centre. Once disembarked from the ferry the guards
bludgeoned them to death with hammers and axes. Around 30,000
Gypsies, more than at Auschwitz, were despatched at Jasenovac.

A Norwegian prisoner remembers children arriving at Sachsenhausen
from Ravensbruck on 4 March 1945: 'They were Gypsy children,
amazingly beautiful and delightful but starving. They were musicians. In
Block 16, the Norwegian block, we fed them and in return they gave us
a concert.'

Rudolph Kustermeir wrote of the last days of Bergen-Belsen, when
order had broken down: 'There were always violins and guitars in the
camp and, in the evenings, Gypsies would play a little. Towards the end,
encouraged by the SS who gave them cigarettes, they suddenly formed
an orchestra and played from morning to night while bodies were being
tumbled into the ground and the guards rained down blows on the

hapless prisoners in time to the tunes of Lehar and Johann Strauss. The Gyspies even played throughout the night; no-one could sleep. We were stretched out in our barracks; the Gypsies came and went playing snatches of this and that and receiving small presents in return. They came in to our barracks around 11.00pm, then at 2.00am and again at 5.00am. Some prisoners objected that this was madness; others were only too happy to have some distraction.'

But the Romany musicians and singers had a further role: to keep up the morals of their own people with songs that evoked a happier past and gave hope of freedom in the future. Ceija Stojka, a survivor of Auschwitz, speaks of the songs sung in the camp, many of them from before the war but others, like 'We have reached the paradise of Auschwitz' sung to the tune of 'Lili Marlene', written at the time. Only a handful have survived, most, presumably, having perished with the singers.

After 1945, Gypsies did not want to speak of what they had suffered. They had been forced to break their own code on food, hygiene and relations between the sexes. For most survivors, it was better to draw a veil over the Nazi era. Moreover, there are few first-hand accounts from Rom and Sinti survivors, not only because many were illiterate, but because, after the war, most found themselves living under communist regimes that discouraged the use of Romany. Rather than publish their memories in the official state language, they chose silence.

The Hungarian Roma poet Karoly Bari recalls: 'In their improvised songs, survivors never mentioned the torture of the camps perhaps because they could not find adequate words. When they did refer to the camps, it was always in a dry, objective way... When it is a question of links between a dead person and those close to him, traditional laments speak of messages passing between them carried by birds.' Bari quotes one of these songs: *Ciriklori, ciriklori/Ingar hiro de kathar/Ingar hiro, ke darava...* Little bird, little bird/Carry my message/Carry the message that I am afraid...

Of over 20,000 Romanies deported to Auschwitz, possibly as few as 1,000 survived. The following song was sung by the Czech Ruzena Danielova in Auschwitz where her husband and all five children died.

[Deportee's lover] In Auschwitz there is a great house/Where my beloved sits/Sits and thinks/And forgets me

[Prisoner] Little black bird/Take my letter/Take it to my wife/To tell

her I am a prisoner here in Auschwitz

In Auschwitz we are starving/With nothing to eat/Not even a crust/And the boss of our Block is an evil man.

Every day he beats us/And forces us to work./If he takes a fancy to a girl, he takes her off/And orders her: sleep there.

The day I leave here and return home/I'll kill our boss.

A generation has grown up since 1945 almost entirely ignorant of the ordeal of their Roma relations, who neither sing of it nor tell stories and who, in most cases, cannot write. It's only recently that survivors have begun to speak of what happened to them and that a new generation of poets and singers have begun to take the Holocaust as their subject. '*Auschwitz-ate hi kherbaro*', along with the few songs to have survived that time, may be seen as the monument to the forgotten victims. ❏

Donald Kenrick is a former honorary secretary of the British Gypsy Council and was official interpreter at three World Romany Congresses. Some of the episodes in this article are from his Gypsies under the Swastika *(University of Hertfordshire Press, UK 1995)*

EGYPT

The Devil has the best PR
Peter Snowdon

In January 1997, 78 teenagers were arrested in early-morning raids in Cairo and Alexandria. Police informed media that the suspects were guilty of devil-worshipping, distributing guns to the poor, drinking the blood of rats, practising group sex and digging up corpses in the Commonwealth Cemetery. They were also big heavy metal fans. Once the press campaign was stripped away, however, little remained but T-shirts printed with 'strange designs', CDs and concert tickets. All other allegations proved groundless. So why the fuss? The government had just celebrated the start of *Ramadan* by executing a number of alleged Islamist terrorists, following this up with a wave of arrests in Upper Egypt. How better to re-establish its pious credentials than by targeting a godless western 'cult' that was perverting the children of the elite — most of those arrested were students at the American University? It was a nice plan, doomed to failure. As one police officer admitted, most of the youths he interrogated 'don't really know what Satanism is.'

GEORGE MCKAY

'This filthy product of modernity...'

Jazz is the music of real as well as romantic ideas of freedom: the liberating joy of a soaring saxophone solo, the legacy of slavery and racial oppression, the ecstatic sexuality of 'Jazz Age' dancing, the relationship between 1960s free jazz and the Civil Rights movement in the United States.

It's an American music spanning what Gertrude Stein called the American century. Just as significantly, however, jazz is about the effort to create indigenous forms, to blend its focus on improvisation with local musical and cultural practice. Jazz has an international profile, its own diasporic narrative: in Europe, folk forms from the gypsy jazz of the Hot Club of France to the Bulgarian wedding music of Ivo Papasov have reinvented themselves through jazz. Yet because jazz is such an identifiably American form of music, even at its most global, throughout the century it has been an element in state power struggles. As a US cultural export, jazz has frequently found itself used as both a weapon and a target in ideological wars.

Jazz was one of the cultural battlegrounds for authoritarian regimes in World War II and the Cold War. While the Marxist critic Theodor Adorno railed against jazz and popular music alike as 'standardising' forms that made 'rhythmically obedient' 'pseudo-individuals' of their listeners, Maxim Gorky railed against 'this insulting chaos of mad sounds'. During World War II, jazz was prohibited or discouraged in Japan, Germany, Italy and the Soviet Union.

That it was music played by American blacks and Jews – let alone by European Gypsies like Django Rheinhardt – was justification enough for Nazi hatred. 'Negrodom, the art of the subhuman' was Goebbels's judgement. While Hitler was refusing to shake the hand of black sprinter

Jesse Owens at the 1936 Berlin Olympics, leading American jazz
musicians were being banned from performing in the country. There
were musical justifications too: because of its syncopated rhythms, jazz
couldn't be marched to, for example. Adorno was wrong: jazz rhythms
were feared for their disobedience.

Although, as Michael H Kater writes in *Different Drummers: Jazz in
the Culture of Nazi Germany*, 'despite all the polemics, jazz would never
be officially banned', regional crackdowns on live performance, as well as
centralised censorship of radio and the recording industry, were effective
means of silencing. In recognition of the popularity of dance and swing
music, however, the Nazis compromised on the production of light
music.

The Czech writer Josef Skvorecky remembers a set of Nazi
regulations that included the following: 'so-called jazz compositions may
contain at most 10 per cent syncopation; the remainder must consist of a
natural *legato* movement devoid of the hysterical rhythmic reverses
characteristic of the music of the barbarian races and conducive to dark
instincts'. When Skvorecky first wrote of these regulations in
Czechoslovakia in 1958, the communist censors banned his text.

Yet jazz was also a focus of enthusiasm and identity for anti-Nazi
youth in Germany itself during World War Two. Like punks or hippies
before their time, groups of young Germans dressed and behaved
outrageously in a gesture of defiance against Nazi authority, using as
their subcultural soundtrack American and British swing music. The
Hottjungen ('Swing Youth') groups were so named in clear contrast to the
official Nazi *Hitlerjungen* ('Hitler Youth') movement. Names of groups
and members and the use of western frontier imagery show the US
influence: the Harlem Club, the Cotton Club, Texas Jack, the Al
Capone Gang, the Navajos.

The *Hottjungen* were rebelling against both the war effort and the
dominant Nazi ideology of racial purity. With their long hair,
extravagant clothes, badges, make-up, wild dancing at rave-like parties
and sexual freedom, they were a highly visible subculture in Nazi society.
Some ended up in concentration camps, where jazz bands – like the
'Merry Five' in Auschwitz, for instance – entertained officers who were
supposed to despise such degenerate music. Eric Vogel, a Czech Jew,
played jazz in a concentration camp, literally for his life. Transported to
Dachau, he jumped from the train, dodged machine gun fire, and hid.

Vogel writes powerfully that his first sight of the liberating GIs was a jeep with the words 'BOOGIE-WOOGIE' written on the front: 'I truly and literally had made my living with jazz.'

The sheer pull of jazz music and style has also been felt in other totalitarian regimes, no doubt because of its forbidden nature, but because it connotes pleasure, freedom of expression, sympathy for the oppressed and so on. In the Soviet Union in the 1960s, the *Shtatniki* (after Shtaty – the States) were a group of young intellectuals and artists who listened to jazz, wore American suits and were seen as resisting communist ideology. Both the *Hottjungen* and the *shtatniki* anticipate the US model of hippie counter-culture exported from the 1960s on. But the music their alternative lifestyles revolved around was jazz.

At the same time, the US was using jazz as propaganda. Bandleader and USAF airman Glenn Miller commented on Allied Expeditionary Forces radio towards the end of the World War II: 'America means freedom, and there is no expression of freedom quite so sincere as music!' During the Cold War, too, the potential of jazz as a transmitter of US values such as tolerance, freedom and pleasure, was being fully employed. A 1955 *New York Times* report on the enthusiastic reception of jazz musicians in Europe was headed: 'United States Has Secret Sonic Weapon: Jazz'. Its potential as propaganda was harnessed equally effectively by the other side: in the mid-1950s, for instance, the Polish government was declaring that 'the building of socialism proceeds more lightly and more rhythmically to the accompaniment of jazz'.

Americanisation through culture was part of the Cold War project, and it wasn't just jazz that was part of the propaganda war: overseas exhibitions of the supposedly radical art of Abstract Expressionism were secretly subsidised by the CIA.

What about jazz in Britain? The BBC banned 'hot music' from the airwaves in 1935 and it was not until 1956 that the ban on performances by American musicians was lifted. The ban itself was a result of a stand-off between US and UK unions; in the eyes of some, the ban had racist origins in fears of African-Americans putting British musicians out of work. Unsurprisingly, there was an explosion of interest in jazz, traditional and modern, in the late 1950s. From 1958, the trad jazz revival and the birth of CND were interwoven: music and direct action politics combining against the state. The related skiffle boom was an early form of DiY musical culture, long predating punk rock or acid house. Even before then, as an indirect result of the BBC's reluctance, then refusal, to broadcast hot music, live dance-jazz bands toured the country playing village and church halls in a way that prefigures later underground moments and movements.

Even today, as Stuart Nicholson notes in a 1995 Arts Council *Review of Jazz in England*, 'Cultural integration of jazz within mainstream arts in this country still remains pathetically slow'. Maybe the distaste in the early years of the BBC casts a long shadow. Jazz isn't banned from the BBC today, of course; it just doesn't feature very much. But as the first director general and shaping force of the BBC, Lord Reith, made clear when he heard that the Nazis had banned some jazz broadcasts in the 1930s, this was the right way to deal with 'this filthy product of modernity'. ❏

George McKay *is reader in contemporary cultural studies at the University of Central Lancashire. His most recent book is* DiY Culture: Party and Protest in Nineties Britain *(Verso, 1998)*

Credit: Sally Olding

MARTIN MILLAR

Lily's Man

O n the phone to her big sister Ruby, Lily was gloomy.
'I still can't get used to not going to a football match at the
weekend.'

Admission prices had risen to such an astonishing level that it was
quite likely that Lily would never see her team play again. That was bad
enough, but Lily had spent the last two seasons edging closer to Joseph, a
young man she was very fond of.

'Which was quite difficult since they made the stadium all seater. I
never approved of that legislation. I was much happier standing. Also, it
made it easier getting closer to Joseph.'

'You should have gone on the fans' protest,' said Ruby.

'Are you mad?' replied Lily. 'I have better things to do with my life
than protesting. Anyway the protest fell on the nineteenth day of my hair
cycle and you know how bad my hair looks on day nineteen of the
cycle.'

The problem could have been avoided if only young Lily had moved
quicker, but Lily was shy, not the sort of person to grab a man and ask
him for a date. Besides, she really only felt confident for two or three
days every month, these days being in the middle of her quite complex
hair cycle, when, some days after having it bleached and cut, it had
reached perfection. All too soon, it would plunge back into the cycle of
decline.

'But today is a number one hair day,' she informed Ruby. 'Which is
just as well because at the last football match I could afford I finally
managed to talk to Joseph. He told me he's been working as a road
sweeper to raise some money for a rave he's organising. Tonight I'm
going to borrow the car, find the rave, find Joseph, dance for a while

then bundle him in and drive home sharply.'

'That sounds unusually determined,' said Ruby, admiringly.

'I know. But I haven't had sex for two years and I'm starting to feel the effects.'

Lily was happy. A wave of optimism swept over her. She felt that not only would she meet Joseph tonight, her hair would look really good as well. She spent the day getting ready, borrowed the car from her flatmate Ian, and headed off. She was a little nervous about being in the country but was willing to risk it

'My shyness was getting out of hand. I was in danger of never having sex again. Something had to be done.'

Ruby was surprised to receive a phone around three in the morning from Lily on her mobile.

'What's happening? Are you still dancing?'

'No. Dancing was never an option. The police declared the rave illegal and stopped everyone who was headed there. I spent the night in a big queue of road blocks and traffic jams but I'm not giving up.'

'You're not?'

'Certainly not. Joseph has fled to a travellers' site nearby to stay with friends and I'm heading over that way. I rescued a turntable from the debacle so he's bound to be pleased. If my flatmate phones up looking for his car, tell him you haven't heard from me.'

'Shouldn't you go home and rest for a while?'

'Absolutely not. I am full of energy and what's more I am now quite desperate for sex. And if I don't get into bed with Joseph tonight, who knows when the next chance may come? In another couple of days my hair will be in decline. Meanwhile Joseph might to decide to go to India and then where will I be?'

Ruby shook her head. It seemed that two years of celibacy had driven her little sister into a frenzy.

'Well good luck,' said Ruby. 'Let me know how you're getting on. I'll be up all night working on the cardboard statue.'

Ruby, by hard work and application, had started to make some progress in the art world. If she could produce a really good collection of cardboard statues, she had every chance of a spot in the 'New Artists' exhibition at the Tate Gallery. Consequently she was working all hours of the day and night. Around six in the morning, while she was rummaging around in the fridge for a beer, her sister phoned up in tears.

'I am still in the country lane,' she said. 'They accused me of being part of the Rave conspiracy and they have confiscated the turntable. Are they allowed to do that?'

'I'm afraid they are.'

'Joseph won't be very pleased,' said Lily, sniffing.

She pulled herself together.

'If my flatmate phones up, prepare him for a little damage to the car.'

Lily gamely sped on. As she neared the travellers' site she slowed to check her hair in the mirror. It was still perfect, but she arrived just in time to see Joseph being thrown into a large police wagon along with four other travellers while their vehicles were towed away.

'But we're allowed to be here,' she heard Joseph call. 'This is a designated travellers' site.'

'Was a designated travellers' site, you mean,' said a policeman 'They changed the law.'

Joseph saw Lily standing forlornly by her car.

'Thanks for coming,' he said. 'Could you get me a lawyer?'

On the phone to Ruby, Lily was outraged.

'What is going on here? All I'm trying to do is sleep with Joseph and every time I get near he's getting dragged away by the police. I'll never get a shag at this rate.'

'Are you coming home now?' asked Ruby.

'Not yet. I had to phone for a lawyer to get Joseph out of the police station.'

Ruby was astonished. She wouldn't have imagined her little sister would have known how to phone for a lawyer.

'It was difficult,' admitted Lily. 'But I had one of these little cards saying what to do if you were arrested. The lawyer said he'd have Joseph out soon. I'm going to his new squat to meet him. Maybe there's a positive side to all this trouble. It seems to be bringing us closer together. How's the cardboard statue coming along?'

'Fine,' replied Ruby. 'Except I can't find any cardboard that's quite thick enough for the torso. I'll have to go out looking soon. How is your hair?'

'Still in prime condition,' Lily assured her. 'Irresistible to a man who just spent the night in a police cell, I would have thought.'

The morning sky above was turning autumn grey as Lily, still full of energy, raced back into South London. She arrived just in time to find bailiffs boarding up the windows while two sad-looking inhabitants loaded their belongings into a van.

'Oh no,' cried Lily. 'Have you been evicted already?'

'Afraid so. It's getting impossible to squat these days.'

'What about Joseph?'

'I don't think he'll come back here now. He'll probably go to his friend Mo's flat.'

Lily ground her teeth.

'He's gone again,' she informed Ruby on the phone. 'Kicked out by bailiffs. It is appalling the way the authorities are persecuting this man. I think my eyes are starting to bulge with sexual desire. Is that possible?'

'It's never happened to me. But I never went without sex for two years.'

'It's two years and three months actually,' admitted Lily, sadly.

Ruby was now becoming concerned about her sister's behaviour.

'Can't you wait another day or two?'

'No, I can't. I told you, my eyes are starting to bulge. It's your fault. You were the one who got me to boost my sex drive.'

It was true. Ruby, concerned about her sister's lack of libido, had strongly advised her to have her third chakra seen to and buy a kitten.

'The combination of the opened sex chakra and the aura of caring developed by looking after a kitten will give you both a powerful sex drive and make you pretty much irresistible.'

Apparently it was working.

'If Ian phones about his car, ask him to feed the kitten. Bye.'

Lily roared down the hill to Brixton, heading for Joseph's friend Mo's flat.

'These chakras are really opening up,' she thought, and savagely cut up a Transit van at the traffic lights. Close to Brixton disaster struck when the car ground to a halt. Lily pounded the steering wheel in frustration. The car still refused to move. She called Ruby.

'Did you try pounding the steering wheel?'

'Of course. It didn't do any good. Then I tried that Buddhist chant for the well being of machinery that you used to fix the washing machine but that didn't work either. What'll I do?'

'Did you put petrol in it?'

'What?' said Lily, confused. 'What? What? What?'

'Petrol.'

'Petrol? You think I should?'

'Maybe. Have you checked the dial?'

Lily struggled around inside the car for a while.

'That may be the problem. What's the matter with Ian? Why doesn't he put enough petrol in his car?'

Lily went in search of a garage. This really was serious suffering. It had been bad enough struggling round the country all night without having to walk through Brixton looking for petrol. At the garage she took the precaution of checking her hair in the rest room.

'Still okay,' she muttered, relieved. 'But it can't last for ever.'

She struggled back with a can of petrol only to find the car had been towed away.

'It's a new red route,' explained a not very sympathetic traffic warden. 'You're not allowed to stop here.'

Lily exploded in fury.

'Well how the hell was I meant to know that?'

'There are big red lines painted all over the road.'

'Oh,' said Lily. 'I thought they were for the carnival.'

She left the petrol at the side of the road, crammed her hair supplies into her bag and hurried off to the bus stop. Mo's house was still some way off and she had no desire to walk there and meet Joseph when she was covered in sweat, and maybe with her hair disorganised by the wind. An unusual strength was rising inside her and she felt that she would not be put off by anything. So it was with some disappointment that she realised that she did not have any money for the bus fare. She had spent it all on petrol.

'I'm getting a little fed up with all this,' she thought. 'No wonder I've been celibate for two years and three months. It's practically impossible to fuck anyone in this town.'

Lily was made bold by the circumstances. She held out her hand to passers by.

'Spare change? You got twenty pence?'

No-one seemed to have spare change or twenty pence. Lily fumed.

'Spare change?'

No-one responded.

'I am disgusted with the heartlessness of these people,' thought Lily. 'Can't they see when a woman is desperate?'

'Hey you,' she yelled, grabbing a large man by the gold chain round his neck. 'You got any spare change?'

And so it was that Lily was arrested and thrown into a cell in Brixton police station under the new regulations against aggressive begging, passed only that month by a government keen to make the streets a safer place.

'No jury will convict me,' stated the irate Lily.

'Maybe not,' said the police sergeant, who was disturbingly large beside Lily's small frame. 'But you're not entitled to a jury for this sort of charge.'

Lily was astonished. She had vaguely assumed that you were always entitled to a jury.'

'What about a phone call?' demanded Lily. 'I know I still get a phone call. I saw it on TV.'

Ruby was alarmed to hear of her sister's plight.

'I'll be right there.'

'And can you send a message to Joseph telling him I'll be there soon?'

'I'll call him.'

'Mo doesn't have a phone.'

Ruby said she'd use her initiative. It took some time for her to make her way to the police station in South London and even longer for her to get Lily out of the cell. The duty solicitors were all busy and Ruby was obliged to recruit the help of Patrick, a young law student she knew in the area. It was early evening before formalities were completed.

'I'm sorry it took so long,' said Patrick 'It is shocking the way your human rights have been denied.'

'Right, whatever,' muttered Lily, looking round eagerly for Joseph. She noticed that Ruby's arms were full of cardboard.

'Extra thick,' explained Ruby. 'Just what I need. I picked it up outside the police station. Look, the box says "Riot shields, handle with care".'

'How can you think about art at a time like this? Where is Joseph? Did you get in contact with him?'

'I sent him a message. Patrick's young brother went down to his council estate.'

At that moment a youth was brought struggling into the police station.

'What are you doing with my young brother?' demanded Patrick.

'He's broken the new curfew,' said the policeman who had him in his grasp. 'No one under fifteen is allowed out after dark. It's no use protesting son, we've got your picture all over the video cameras on the estate.'

Lily stood with her mouth open as Patrick's brother was hauled away, followed by Patrick himself, angrily protesting about human rights.

'I just can't believe it. Is there really a curfew?'

Apparently there was.

'Now Joseph didn't get my message. He won't know where I am. What is going on here? At this rate I'll never get into bed with Joseph. I can't take much more of this.'

Ruby was struggling with the cardboard she'd picked up from the street.

'I think we should go home,' she suggested, but her sister refused.

'I will seek out Joseph to the ends of the earth.'

A police car drew up. Joseph emerged, followed by several policemen in plain clothes.

'What happened to you?' wailed Lily.

'Random drug test. I just turned up at work to pick up my wages and they caught me by surprise. I forgot they introduced testing last week.'

'Stoned out of his head,' said the policeman bringing up the rear.

'Disgraceful behaviour, what with him having responsibility for keeping the pavements clean.'

Lily sat down heavily on the pavement which, it was true, was rather dirty.

It started to rain. Lily felt the water trickling through her hair. It was more than five years since rain had touched her hair. She started to cry.

Ruby comforted her.

'Don't cry. Let's go home.'

Lily wiped her eyes. A determined look came to her face.

'I'm not going home,' she declared. 'I haven't come this far to be defeated now. Give me some of that cardboard.'

Lily wrenched a piece of cardboard from Ruby and started writing on it with a pen.

'I'm making a placard. They can't get away with this. I'm going to protest until Joseph is released. You are still allowed to protest right?'

Ruby thought so, as long as they weren't causing an obstruction.

Patrick appeared from the police station. When he saw Lily marching up and down with her placard he was mightily impressed.

'Lily that is wonderful. I never thought you were the sort of person who was prepared to make a stand. I always thought you were just bothered about superficial things like your hair.'

Ruby, seeing that her sister was about to turn violent, stepped in hastily to intervene.

'Well Patrick, you had better take you brother home now before he is arrested again.'

Patrick agreed, but said he would be back immediately to join in Lily's protest.

A large police sergeant appeared beside them. Ruby, Lily and Patrick, by now all quite familiar with the man, looked at him doubtfully.

'I trust you are not planning on hanging around here for too long?' he said, menacingly.

'As long as it takes,' replied Lily, gamely. 'We're still allowed to protest, they haven't made that illegal yet.'

'Unfortunately not,' admitted the policeman. 'But our chief superintendent hates it when people hang around outside the station. It makes him nervous. So nervous that he generally gets to thinking he's being picked on.'

'And?'

'And you can't hang around picking on someone these days, Miss. Not since they made stalking illegal.'

Ruby gasped in astonishment.

'Stalking? I thought they passed that law to protect women who were being followed.'

'That may be,' retorted the sergeant. 'But, funnily enough, we have found it very useful for getting rid of anyone who insists on hanging around where they're not wanted. So if you wouldn't mind just moving on before I am forced to arrest you.'

Ruby and Lily trudged away, defeated at last.

'I think I am injured,' said Lily, morosely. 'My sex chakra has imploded. I'll never be the same woman again. I can't believe what happened to me over the past twenty four hours.'

'Me neither,' agreed Ruby. 'Though at least I got some cardboard.'

'Excuse me Miss,' said the large policeman. 'Would that be our cardboard you are attempting to steal?'

'Steal? I picked it up from your bins.'

'Property in rubbish bins belongs to the original owner until collected by the council. Magistrates can be very tough on people like you. But in the interest of good community relations, I won't press charges. Just put it back where it belongs.'

Ruby dumped the cardboard.

'Your community relations are fabulous,' she said.

They went sadly on their way.

'I am now sick of this country,' said Lily. 'It will take me years to find anyone else I want to sleep with. I am giving up on Joseph. The relationship has plunged into a cycle of destruction. I might have to go abroad. Somewhere where a woman can fully express her sex drive and there is no chance of getting arrested under some repressive law. Where would that be?'

'I'm not sure,' said Ruby. 'How about Ireland?'

'Is Ireland nice?'

'It always looks lovely on the beer commercials.'

Lily studied her hair in her hand mirror for a while.

'You know, I have learned an important lesson tonight.'

'What?' asked Ruby.

'This hair-gel is really good. It has protected my hair in all sorts of difficult situations. Even the rain hasn't ruined it. Were it not for that, my spirit would be crushed.'

'Good,' said Ruby. 'The experience has also helped me. I am full of ideas for new cardboard statues. Speaking as your older sister Lily, I would say it is very important never to let your spirit be crushed.' ❏

Martin Millar's *latest novel is* Love and Peace with Melody Paradise *(IMP Fiction, UK) also see http://dspace.dial.pipex.com/m.millar/*

MARTIN CLOONAN

Massive attack

On 12 January 1991, the day before the United Nations deadline for Saddam Hussein's compliance with its resolution demanding the Iraqi withdrawal from Kuwait ran out, Giles Peterson, a DJ and director of the commercial radio station Jazz FM, played 90 minutes of 'peace music' to show his opposition to war. He also broadcast details of peace marches that were taking place in London that afternoon. As a result, he was sacked. The reason given for this was that the station had received a 'serious complaint' centring on a contravention of the 1990 Broadcasting Act that requires commercial radio stations to be politically impartial. The Radio Authority (which oversees the conduct of commercial radio stations) said the sacking was an internal matter for Jazz FM and thus beyond its remit, but ruled that the station had breached the rules on politically impartiality.

Meanwhile, the BBC had shown its own political allegiance by transferring Radio 1's Simon Bates' show to the Gulf to boost the morale of British troops. While commercial radio was expected to be politically impartial, the BBC used pop to support the actions of 'our boys' in the Gulf.

Once the war started, it was clear that some people at the BBC had decided that listeners' sensibilities back home needed protection. The BBC Radio Training Unit compiled a list of records it believed should be treated with caution for the duration of the war. The list was sent to the BBC's 37 local radio stations and appears to have been an attempt to avoid any offence whatsoever. Thus it included such titles as: ABBA's 'Waterloo', Aha's 'Hunting High and Low', The Bangles' 'Walk Like an Egyptian', Kate Bush's 'Army Dreamers', Jose Feliciano's 'Light My Fire', Lulu's 'Boom Bang A Bang', Nicole's 'A Little Peace' and Tears For Fears' 'Everybody Wants To Rule The World' (*Index* Vol 20, Nos 4/5 1991).

The list attracted much hilarity in the British press and led Tim Neale, Head of Radio Training, to explain that it contained as many tracks as possible with lyrics 'that need thought in scheduling'. It also included instructions on how to exclude them from the computer which holds selections for each show. Neale emphasised that the decision on what to include and exclude was left to programmers and presenters and insisted that, contrary to press reports, there was no ban merely 'an attempt to save ... some time and ensure proper care is taken not to cause unnecessary offence'. However, it is clear that the list became a *de facto* ban for the duration of the war.

While it is clear that the war was a sensitive issue that some listeners did not want to be reminded of when they were listening to music stations which are essentially escapist in nature, the BBC pursued its desire not to be offensive to an extraordinary degree. Thus The Rolling Stones's 'High Wire' single, which criticised the arms trade and was released around the time of the war, did not receive the amount of Radio 1 plays it might have expected. Johnny Beerling, head of Radio 1, told the *Sunday Times* that playing the record would lead to the press proclaiming 'another case of the leftie BBC supporting the enemies of freedom'. Tory MP Sir John Stokes called the record appalling at a time of war and asked why the band couldn't do something in a more jingoistic vein.

The potential for offence is shown by the case of Paper Lace's 'Billy Don't Be A Hero'. Originally a UK number one hit in 1974, it tells the story of a soldier who is killed after showing the sort of bravery in battle his sweetheart had implored him not to prior to his leaving home. While the song is vaguely anti-war, at any other time the record would have attracted comment only for its inanity. However, when it was played on Radio 1 (on Bates' show) just after a Gulf war news bulletin, it attracted 110 complaints. This illustrates one of the major characteristics of censorship: its historically contingent nature which ties it to contemporary events. A text which at other times would have been totally innocuous was potentially offensive during wartime.

Other records also failed to make the station's playlist or were amended because of the war. Carter The Unstoppable Sex Machine's 'Bloodsports For All' – a critique of racism in the army – was vetoed by the BBC and the band flipped the 'B' side of the single, 'Bedsitter' to become the 'A' side. The Happy Mondays had to omit the lines 'Gonna build an airforce place/Gonna blow up your race' from 'Loose Fit' to get plays; The KLF had to edit out the samples of machine gun fire from their '3 AM Eternal' single. The band Massive Attack were referred to as Massive until the war ended and Tim Simenon reverted to his own name rather than use his normal moniker of Bomb The Base. It was also reported that the commercial Radio Victory in Portsmouth had banned Blondie's 'Island of Lost Souls' for the duration of the conflict.

With hindsight, these restrictions seem amusing, facile even. This begs the question of why they were implemented. It is clear that the BBC was nervous after years of political attacks from a hostile government that perceived the organisation as the embodiment of the liberal establishment it detested. Beerling's remarks show this. The BBC was also keen to have its Charter renewed around this time and reluctant to rock the political boat. Thus the desire not to offend listeners is better read as a desire not to offend government, although some genuine concern not to cause listeners offence can also be seen.

However, the restrictions on popular music can also be read as part of a concerted attempt to build a pro-war consensus, in effect to manufacture consent. Dissident voices were stifled and potentially embarrassing pop lyrics curtailed. Other than Musicians Against The War, who organised an anti-war sing in, nothing was heard from pop's anti-war tradition. Pop was presented as part of a consensus that either supported or wanted to ignore the war. ❑

Martin Cloonan is the author of Banned! – Censorship of Popular Music in Britain: 1967-92 *(Arena 1996)*

MARTIN CLOONAN

Aunty at war

In all the wars in which the UK has been involved since the foundation of the BBC in 1923, the Corporation has been under tremendous pressure not to give succour to the enemy. By the time WWII broke out, the BBC was well established and in a position to act as government mouthpiece and national unifier. This role included controlling the transmission of popular culture, including music.

Throughout the war, the BBC vetoed the playing of overtly Germanic music and Wagner was effectively banned. The works of Alan Bush, a Marxist composer, were also banned for a time. The song 'Deep in the Heart of Texas' was also vetoed on the grounds that munitions workers too often downed tools to join in the requisite clapping.

After the war, the BBC continued to exercise control over the airwaves. It resisted early rock'n'roll and supported government action to outlaw pirate radio. In 1967, the creation of Radio 1 gave it its own pop station. By the time commercial radio was licensed to broadcast in the UK in 1973, the tradition of radio subordinating itself to the state when required to was well established.

Since then, the longest-running area of censorship has been in the coverage of events in Northern Ireland. Records vetoed by the BBC include Wings' 'Give Ireland Back to the Irish' and McGuiness Flint's anti-internment song 'Let the People Go'. After the government ban on broadcasting IRA/Sinn Fein spokespeople or any support for terrorism, the Pogues' track 'Birmingham Six', which dealt with the imprisonment of innocent 'terrorists', was banned by the Independent Broadcasting Authority. That Petrol Emotion also had their 'Cellophane' single banned. The ban also prevented the journalist Paul Foot from playing his favourite song, 'Kelly the Boy From Killane' on the commercial station LBC. ❏

MC

YEHUDI MENUHIN

A suitable case for censorship

When Index last devoted an issue to banned music Yehudi Menuhin called for an end to Muzak, in vain it seems. He returns to the fray

I could circle the thorny centre of the argument, but I shall plunge into the brambles. There is a case to be made for restricting certain types of musical activity – as there is for regulating other potent human drives.

In an ideal world, it should be possible to protect people from 'music' injurious to the ear, soul and sensibility. Such music – more muzak – is the deadening refrain piped into lifts, arcades, restaurants and aircraft to a captive audience who must be abused in this fashion without consultation. I would dearly like to see (and hear) some system for regulating these unwelcome broadcasts by restricting the financial gain of those operators who exploit both music and the hapless consumers of their product.

Why can there not be zones of silence prescribed, as now exist near hospitals, where one is free of man-made, mechanical, recorded or amplified noise, or those degenerate soundwaves that pass for music? Today we regulate drugs, food, films and think it right to do so. Why can there not exist similar proscriptions on the infliction of *ersatz* music, which is no less open to abuse?

There are, of course, certain types of real music which are censored – and this is in itself a token of its power. This has been recognised by governments and philosophers since the time of Plato. Music in some regimes has charms only when it conforms to the propaganda of the day; in these regimes it is not art but power that is music to the ears. I remember in Russia, in 1945, hearing an oratorio, for that is what it was, in praise of Lenin. Again, in China, until recently, music and musicians suffered considerably under the Gang of Four.

Credit: Rex

Commercial interest and tyrants: both attempt the censorship of music, the former by harnessing its potency for financial gain, the latter for the consolidation of their own power.

I wrote the words above in 1983; in 1998, things have only got worse. Every possible crevasse of silence is being shattered with noise, polluting our environment. And there is also meaningless noise which conveys no message whatsoever: the sirens of the emergency services need not be such sounds of terror and panic; they could be the alternating notes in thirds used in Paris. The sound is used to warn us to clear the path for the ambulance or the fire engine, but it need not convey the emotive state of anguish of those directly involved in the heart attack or the fire. Even the paramedics in the ambulance are supposed to be cool, precise and efficient. How can that be when they are assaulted by blood-curdling noise? ❏

Yehudi Menuhin, *the well-known violinist, is a patron of Index on Censorship*

The Gold Standard of Literary Annoyance

ABRASIVENESS. Where would contemporary cultural criticism be without it? At THE BAFFLER, it's the quality that inclines us to accentuate the negative and cast the shining future in gray, depressing tones. We pack every issue with a full payload of gibes, rants and smug contumely. That's why we've become the last word in grating prose, in every hall of learning and site of Web, great or small.

We happen to think that abrasiveness is a quality worth hanging around for. And we hope you join us to ride out the twilight years of the American Century.

Featured in BAFFLER Number Eleven, "Middletown Delenda Est":

Thomas Frank unmasks the bogus populism of "public journalism":
"Soon after deciding to tear down the wall between editorial and business in a quest to make the Los Angeles Times more profitable, publisher Mark Willes announced that in order to make female readers 'feel like the paper's theirs,' it needed to come up with stories that were 'more emotional, more personal, less analytical.' Wherever newspaper moguls talk populism and profits simultaneously, it seems, the practical results take the same form: a sort of middle-class relativism in which tenaciously held ideas are the greatest journalistic anathema of all."

Paul Maliszewski pranks the lesser lights of American business journalism:
"I set out to translate the text of a torture manual used at the School of the Americas into the language and rhetoric of a manager's how-to. With very few changes – substituting 'employee' for 'subject,' for instance – the piece began to look more and more like a business advice column. Now published and with nothing to announce it as a satire, it lies in wait, looking and reading like just another article. In the Business Journal it is oddly at home."

Marc Cooper recounts his escape from Pinochet's coup:
"We slumped back to the apartment, which soon shook with an enormous thud. Then another. From the second-floor balcony we could see two tanks squatting comfortably in the park, lobbing artillery rounds across the river into the fine arts campus of the University of Chile. That's how the armed forces were restoring order."

You can orderTHE BAFFLER from us directly. Write us at:

P.O. Box 378293, Chicago, IL 60637.

A single issue costs US$6.00, and a four-issue subscription costs US$20.00. Residents of Canada and Mexico are asked to add $1 per issue for postage; all others must add $7 per issue (i.e., $28 extra for a subscription). Make checks payable to THE BAFFLER in US dollars drawn on a US bank. Or ask for the magazine at your local bookstore. Be persistent – they won't believe there's a magazine called "THE BAFFLER."

ROGER WALLIS & GEORGE KLIMIS

Key to the highway

**Record company mergers and intense commercial pressures
are making life difficult for existing stars and wannabees alike**

Music censorship did not end with the fall of communism and the
decline of totalitarian regimes around the world. On the contrary,
it is alive and well – some would say flourishing – in the 'free' world.
What has changed is the driving force behind it: greed as opposed to
fear; economic rather than political considerations.

Take a medium such as television. It is very difficult for a
programmer of a musical TV station to play a video clip that might
alienate the sponsors of the show even if the song has proved its
popularity with the audience. Companies do not want to be associated
with certain artists or songs and the marketing department could
threaten to withdraw their advertising funds. In our interviews with a
music channel it was made clear that the channel 'sells space for
advertising and targets specific demographics' and therefore does not play
everything the record companies or artists release. In a panel discussion
between record labels and various music channels at PopKomm 1996,
the channels went so far as to demand a preview of the video clip before
the company decided to shoot it. This was the response to the German
recording industry which was watching its investment in videos
disappear into thin air when the TV stations would not play them.
Various earlier examples of this practice survive from the famous Ed
Sullivan Show where Elvis Presley was filmed from the waist up, or the
Rolling Stones changing 'Let's spend the night together' to 'Let's spend
some time together'.

A typical example of economic-based censorship has been provided
by the Wal-Mart retail chain in the USA. It might be owned by a
Mormon family but its policy on selling CDs would appear to be driven

more by economic considerations than by religious ones; the same chain stores sell guns. In fact it was the lyrics 'Watch our children kill each other with a gun they bought at Wal–Mart discount stores' that made the chain refuse to stock an album by Sheryl Crow after attempts to persuade the artist to change the lyrics failed. The chain also withdrew Prodigy's 'Smack my bitch up' after it had reputedly sold 150,000 copies without a single customer complaining. With 2,300 stores and nearly 10 per cent of the CDs sold in the US market through their stores, they are a force to be reckoned with. Of course it would be premature to convict the chain of censorship just because it wants to protect its 'credibility capital'. The moral majority that comprises its clientele could easily be offended and the store could, therefore, justify their action on those terms.

It would be wrong, though, to assume that censorship is not welcomed by the record companies. On the contrary, a censorship act sometimes proves to be the best marketing device to promote and 'break' an artist. Just remember Sex Pistols' 'God Save the Queen' which was banned by BBC Radio One when released by Virgin Records. The band had been dropped by both EMI and A&M but both companies denied that they censored the group. Virgin Records, a young company then, made a killing with the Sex Pistols album through the free publicity in the press and the word of mouth that the happenings generated.

Some could cite that incident as a perfect example of market forces working for the benefit of the public and rendering any censorship act obsolete. In a free market, consumers can always get their hands on the goods they want because there is competition between suppliers. Indeed, in the 1960s, when there were more medium-sized recording companies – and maybe more competition for songs and performers – artists such as Bob Dylan could find companies like CBS to record their quasi-revolutionary songs. CBS is now owned by Sony. EMI acquired Virgin in the early-1990s in what was termed the 'sale of the century', thereby changing the competitive landscape. With Seagram taking over Polygram – the result of the Philips/Polydor/Decca amalgamation in the 1970s and 1980s – we are left with five companies controlling around 80 per cent of the world's repertoire.

Another example of making concessions in return for the support of the powerful is the case of Interscope records. In late 1995, the two heads of the campaign against offensive rock lyrics, as well as Senator Robert Dole, criticized Time Warner's policy of releasing gangsta rap, a genre of music that contains explicit lyrics. The target was Interscope, a small label that releases Tupac Shakur, Dr Dre and Snoop Doggy Dogg – all gangsta rap acts. Warner was also criticized in 1992 when it released Ice-T's 'Cop Killer', a song the artist withdrew from the Warner Music Group (WMG) to be released by a different label.

WMG sold its 50 per cent stake in Interscope in October 1995, even though some of WMG's executives thought that Interscope could easily become WMG's fourth major label in the USA. The stake was sold back to Interscope who eagerly awaited the opportunity to get back the shares in order to negotiate better distribution terms with the other majors who were lining up to get a piece of the action.

The incident was critical for Time Warner at the time, since its vested interests in the regulated cable industry prevented it standing up to a powerful man such as Dole. As for the bottom line, it was mildly hurt: with revenues of US$85m, Interscope barely represented 2 per cent of the total music division revenue of US$4bn and a fraction of the US$15bn of the total Time Warner empire's revenues.

This move not only hurt WMG's market share but also its reputation and credibility capital among other stakeholders such as the employees and, more important, the artists.

One of the remedies to the forms of restraint implicit in increasing concentration of ownership, say the free marketers, is the Internet. The concentration of the industry in the hands of the few is not really threatening since the Internet offers the possibility of global self-publishing, bypassing record labels, regulatory regimes and the gatekeepers of conventional media. Without wishing to destroy the utopian dream so carefully crafted by the media on the possibilities of the WWW, it's worth pointing to two important caveats:

The Internet only reaches the haves, not the have–nots. Internet banking is a good example: the few with access to computers and networks, and the money to pay for the various fees can enjoy privileged access to information and services globally. The haves can also shop for the best prices whereas the have–nots must be content with the traditional brick and mortar stores in the USA. Unless there is some provision for universal access, society will be polarised between those two 'communities';

A bigger threat comes with the need for artists to get paid for their music and actually make a living out of it. If they seek financial rewards then they will have to join the system which is comprised of networks of databases where, in the interests of efficiency, ID numbers are assigned to each individual. This makes tracking artists all too easy and abuse of this power will be detrimental to them.

We don't want to smother the Internet in a wet blanket, but any naive view of this new communications animal can allow the inexperienced to walk straight into the arms of a cunning censor. The dilemma for musicians is that if they hope to develop a living via copyright income from music distributed on-line, then they will have to accept being embraced by a global system of registration, collection and distribution. This can be used to support the individual 'case for fair remuneration', but also to allow a strengthening of commercial and government interests' control over this unmanaged network. ❑

Roger Wallis is the director of the Multimedia Research Group at City University Business School, London. He is also a composer and a member of the Board of the Swedish Copyright Collection Society
George Klimis is currently completing a PhD on the future structure of the music industry in a digital, networked environment

USA

It's a knock-out
Randip Panesar

Cassius Clay. Who? A little known fact about heavyweight Muhammad Ali is that he cut what may qualify as the world's first rap album back in 1963. 'I am the Greatest' acquired minor cult status when it was pulled from the shelves by Columbia after Clay's high-profile conversion to Nation of Islam and his related name change in 1964. Unlike rap, Ali's lyrics were hardly incendiary: what propelled the pull was race. Clay had been a multi-million dollar industry, supported by middle class, working class, black and white alike. To have this all-American icon demonstrate solidarity with black separatism and Islam, against a background of civil rights marches, without being whupped in the ring was 'challenging'. Where Clay had stayed silent, Ali shouted. As for the quality of the album, the titles – punctuated by end-of-round bells – say it all. Round I: 'I am the Greatest'; Round 2: 'I am the double Greatest'; and Round 3: 'Do you have to ask?'.